# Contents

# What Is a Noun?

A **noun** can name a **person**, **place**, or **thing**. Look at the examples below.

| Examples of Nouns | |
| --- | --- |
| **Person** | *Lisa, Mr. Rizzo, girl, doctor, student, teacher, neighbor* |
| **Place** | *United States, Maine, Houston, beach, school, bedroom* |
| **Thing** | *rock, tree, pencil, ear, snowflake, sky, scarf, snake* |

1. Circle the **nouns** in each group of words.

   a) road   sing   television   pretty   tulip   frog   quickly   tripped

   b) write   slow   shiny   uncle   spilled   drank   banana   dentist

   c) sweater   computer   difficult   office   friend   soft   sang   hoped

   d) friendly   chocolate   jumped   desk   long   bathtub   architect   Richmond

   e) swimming   kitchen   slowly   crystal   crawling   mountain   officer

2. Circle all the **nouns** in each sentence.

   a) Mrs. Lupino picked ripe tomatoes from the garden in her backyard.

   b) The park was full of noisy children playing in the snow.

   c) Ali and his parents flew to France in an airplane.

   d) My father took the cake out of the refrigerator when the guests arrived.

   e) Use a pencil or a pen to write your answers to the questions.

   f) Please go to the grocery store to pick up some fruits and vegetables.

3. Fill in the blanks with a noun. Then circle whether the noun names a **person**, **place**, or **thing.**

   a) ___________________ is my best friend.
      person    place    thing

   b) I love to go shopping at ___________________.
                         person    place    thing

   c) My favorite restaurant is ___________________.
                         person    place    thing

4. Read the following paragraph. Three have been done for you.

   **Underline** the nouns that name a **person**.
   **Circle** the nouns that name a **place**.
   Put a **box** around the nouns that name a **thing**.

   Sandy enjoys walking her dog on Clark Street and in the park. She wants to start a dog-walking service in the neighborhood. Sandy asks her mother if she knows any neighbors who might be interested. They talk to Mrs. Garcia down the street and Sandy explains her idea. Mrs. Garcia says she needs help walking her dog, and Sandy has her first customer! Mom helps Sandy put a sign on the front lawn that says "Dog Walking Service." Mr. Jones comes by and asks Sandy to come to his house on Mill Street on Tuesdays. Other neighbors come by, too. Now Sandy is a very busy girl. She walks eight dogs every week!

5. Write four sentences that contain at least **three nouns**. Include in your sentences at least one **person**, one **place**, and one **thing**.

________________________________________________________________

________________________________________________________________

________________________________________________________________

________________________________________________________________

________________________________________________________________

________________________________________________________________

________________________________________________________________

________________________________________________________________

________________________________________________________________

________________________________________________________________

________________________________________________________________

________________________________________________________________

# Common Nouns and Proper Nouns

A **noun** names a person, place, or thing.

A **common noun** names a person, place, or thing that is **not specific**.

A **proper noun** names a **specific** person, place, or thing. Proper nouns always start with **capital letters**. Look at the examples below.

| Common Nouns | Examples of Proper Nouns |
| --- | --- |
| girl | Sally, Alana |
| city | New York, Tulsa |
| mall | Millcreek Mall, Lakewood Center |

1. Think about the examples of proper nouns in each row, and write a **common noun** that fits the examples. The first row is completed for you.

| Common Nouns | Examples of Proper Nouns |
| --- | --- |
| a) country | Australia, France, Brazil |
| b) | Mars, Jupiter, Venus |
| c) | Maple Avenue, Main Street |
| d) | Dr. Gupta, Dr. Jones, Dr. Cortes |
| e) | March, May, November |

2. Correct the sentences below by making the **proper nouns** start with **capital letters**.

a) Has marco always lived on poplar road?

_________________________________________________

b) I heard that the mayo clinic is one of the best hospitals in the united states.

_________________________________________________

c) The library closest to me is queens library.

_________________________________________________

d) In june, dr. williams will travel to greece.

_______________________________________________

e) Will astronauts visit neptune and saturn one day?

_______________________________________________

f) My friend josie is raising money for the cancer society in the month of may.

_______________________________________________

g) the natural history museum is a great place to learn about dinosaurs.

_______________________________________________

h) eagle elementary school is located in eagle, idaho.

_______________________________________________

3. Circle whether the noun below is a **common noun** or a **proper noun**.

| | | |
|---|---|---|
| a) dog | *common noun* | *proper noun* |
| b) Rover | *common noun* | *proper noun* |
| c) mall | *common noun* | *proper noun* |
| d) Mall of America | *common noun* | *proper noun* |
| e) girl | *common noun* | *proper noun* |
| f) Lily | *common noun* | *proper noun* |
| g) Sammy | *common noun* | *proper noun* |
| h) city | *common noun* | *proper noun* |
| i) boy | *common noun* | *proper noun* |
| j) Chicago | *common noun* | *proper noun* |

# Exploring Proper Nouns

A **proper noun** names a **specific** person, place, or thing. Proper nouns always start with **capital letters**.

Remember to use capital letters for the types of proper nouns shown below.

| | Examples of Proper Nouns |
|---|---|
| Names of **countries, states,** and **cities** | *Africa, Georgia, Portland* |
| Names of **holidays** | *Labor Day, Valentine's Day* |
| Names of **people** and **pets** | *Frank, Dr. Green, Fluffy, Aunt Rachel, Grandma* |
| Names of **days of the week** and **months of the year** | *Wednesday, September* |
| Names of **businesses, organizations,** and **museums** | *Big Burger, American Red Cross, Natural History Museum* |

1. Correct the sentences below by making the **proper nouns** start with **capital letters**.

   a) We bought a kitten at greenville pet store last tuesday.

   _______________________________________________________

   b) On mother's day, uncle george came from maine to visit us.

   _______________________________________________________

   c) Last april, mrs. alvarez took our class to the alamo in san antonio, texas.

   _______________________________________________________

   d) My aunt and uncle usually spend new year's day in columbus, ohio.

   _______________________________________________________

2. Correct the sentences below by adding **capital letters** to proper nouns. Remember that proper nouns name **specific** people, places, or things.

   a) I have seen many mountains, but I like the rocky mountains the best.

   _______________________________________________________________

   b) the peace bridge links the united states with canada.

   _______________________________________________________________

   c) aunt amy says that bighorn river in montana is a great place for fishing.

   _______________________________________________________________

   d) The maine sluggers is mr. johnson's favorite baseball team.

   _______________________________________________________________

3. Write an example of each type of proper noun.

   a) name of holiday _________________________________

   b) name of a pet _________________________________

   c) name of a day of the week _________________________________

   d) name of a business _________________________________

   e) name of a country _________________________________

   f) name of an organization _________________________________

   g) name of a city _________________________________

4. Read the paragraph below. Highlight the **proper nouns** that should be capitalized. Rewrite the paragraph correctly on the lines below.

Sylvia and bob were on summer vacation. In school, they had learned all about planets such as jupiter and mars. Their moms decided to take them to the california science center so they could learn more. Bob and sylvia lived in san diego, california. They had to drive all the way to los angeles, california, to get to the california science center. It was worth the drive. Everyone had a great day, and sylvia and bob even got to pick something from the gift shop!

# Making Nouns Plural

To make many **nouns** plural, just add the letter **s**.

*Examples: rock – rocks     window – windows     cat – cats     flower – flowers*

For some nouns, you need to do something different. Watch for nouns like the ones below.

| Nouns ending with… | To make the noun plural… |
| --- | --- |
| **s, x, ch,** or **sh** | Add **es** <br> *Example: one fox – two foxes* |
| **Consonant + y** | Change the **y** to **i** and add **es** <br> *Example: one fly — two flies* |

Use plurals of the nouns below to complete the sentences. Use each noun only once. Choose a noun that makes sense in the sentence.

**radish   speech   box   boss   dish   butterfly   bus   puppy   pony**

a) Larry carried the heavy _________________ to the living room.

b) There were two broken _________________ on the kitchen floor.

c) Which of these _________________ will take me downtown?

d) Two speakers gave long _________________ at the event.

e) The cook sliced _________________ to put in the salads.

f) Our dog Coco has six newborn _________________.

g) The _________________ had very colorful wings.

h) The _________________ told the workers to work harder.

i) Andrew has three _________________ in his farm set.

   © Chalkboard Publishing

# Tricky Plural Nouns

Making some nouns plural is tricky!

Be careful when making plurals from nouns that end with the letter *o*.

For some nouns that end with *o*, add the letters *es*.

For other nouns that end with *o*, just add the letter *s*.

| Add *es* | Add *s* | |
| --- | --- | --- |
| volcano – volcanoes | patio – patios | video – videos |
| potato – potatoes | photo – photos | zero – zeros |
| tomato – tomatoes | piano – pianos | solo – solos |

1. Complete each sentence by writing a **plural noun** from the lists above. In each sentence, use a word that makes sense.

   a) My big brother is cutting two _______________ to go on the burgers.

   b) The number eight million has six ____________.

   c) Alex and I picked up two ____________ to watch this weekend.

   d) The new song was playing on all the ____________ in the store.

2. Rewrite each sentence below to make the **underlined nouns** plural. **Do not** use the words **a** or **an** before a plural noun.

   a) We watched a <u>video</u> about a <u>volcano</u> erupting.

   _______________________________________________________________

   b) We weighed a <u>potato</u>, but the scale showed only a <u>zero</u>.

   _______________________________________________________________

   c) Kelly played a <u>solo</u> on a <u>piano</u> on a <u>patio</u>.

   _______________________________________________________________

# Tricky Plural Nouns (continued)

Don't be tricked by tricky **plural nouns**!

For most nouns ending with the letters *fe*, change the *f* to a *v* and add *s*.

*Examples: knife – knives     life – lives     wife – wives*

To make these nouns plural, do not change anything!

*Examples: one fish – two fish     one sheep – six sheep     one deer – four deer*

You will need to remember these tricky plurals.

| Singular | Plural |
| --- | --- |
| child | children |
| foot | feet |
| goose | geese |
| man | men |

| Singular | Plural |
| --- | --- |
| mouse | mice |
| person | people |
| tooth | teeth |
| woman | women |

3. Complete each sentence by writing a **plural noun** shown above.

   a) The flock of _______________ honked loudly as they flew by.

   b) Lots of ____________ live in our attic in winter.

   c) I saw three _______________ eating grass in the forest.

4. Rewrite these sentences to make the **underlined nouns** plural. **Do not** use the words *a* or *an* before a plural noun.

   a) A <u>child</u> can see a <u>mouse</u> hiding in the long grass.

   ________________________________________________

   b) A <u>wife</u> made lots of food for a <u>person</u> at the party.

   ________________________________________________

   c) A <u>woman</u> went to see a <u>sheep</u> at the fair.

   ________________________________________________

Watch out when making plurals from nouns that end with the letter *f*.

For most nouns that end with *f*, change the *f* to a *v* and add **es**.

For a few nouns that end with *f*, just add the letter **s**.

| Change *f* to *v* and add *es* | | Just add *s* | |
|---|---|---|---|
| elf – elves | shelf – shelves | chef – chefs | fluff — fluffs |
| half – halves | thief – thieves | chief – chiefs | roof – roofs |
| leaf – leaves | wolf – wolves | cliff – cliffs | scarf – scarfs |
| loaf – loaves | | cuff – cuffs | spoof – spoofs |

5. Complete each sentence by writing **plural nouns** from the lists above. In each sentence, use a word that makes sense.

a) Three _______________ climbed up the _________ to steal the golden sword.

b) Two _________ howled at the _________ with the pointy ears.

c) Grandma knits _____________ when the _________ turn color in fall.

6. Rewrite these sentences to make the **underlined nouns** plural. **Do not** use the words *a* or *an* before a plural noun.

a) The boys laughed at a <u>spoof</u> of their favorite movie.

_________________________________________________

b) The <u>chief</u> ate an apple <u>half</u>.

_________________________________________________

c) A big <u>fluff</u> is rolling across the living room floor.

_________________________________________________

# Singular Possessive Nouns

A **possessive noun** shows who or what something belongs to.

Add an **apostrophe + s** to a **singular noun** to show belonging.

Below are three examples of **singular possessive nouns**.

| | Singular Possessive Nouns |
|---|---|
| *the bike that belongs to the girl* | *the **girl's** bike* |
| *the computer that belong to Liam* | ***Liam's** computer* |
| *the pages of the book* | *the **book's** pages* |

Rewrite each sentence. Use a **singular possessive noun** to replace the **underlined words** in each sentence.

a) The legs <u>of the table</u> were wobbly.

_______________________________________________

b) The coat <u>that belongs to Abdul</u> got wet in the rain.

_______________________________________________

c) The chirping <u>of the bird</u> woke me up.

_______________________________________________

d) Will you help me find the lid <u>of the container</u>?

_______________________________________________

e) The books <u>that belong to Anna</u> are on the shelf.

_______________________________________________

# Plural Possessive Nouns

Most **plural nouns** end with **s**. Add an **apostrophe after the s** to make a **possessive plural noun**. Below are some examples.

| | Plural Possessive Nouns |
|---|---|
| the gloves that belong to the boys | the **boys'** gloves |
| the headlights of the cars | the **cars'** headlights |
| the cries of the babies | the **babies'** cries |

1. Write the **plural possessive noun** for each example below.

   a) the dog that belongs to my neighbors        my _________________ dog

   b) the roots of the trees        the _________________ roots

   c) the noise of the airplanes        the _________________ noise

Some **plural nouns** do not end with **s**.
*Examples: children   women   men   people*

Add an **apostrophe + s** to turn these plural nouns into **plural possessive nouns.**
*Examples: children's   women's   men's   people's*

2. Rewrite each sentence. Use a **plural possessive noun** to replace the **underlined words** in each sentence.

   a) The coats <u>that belong to the women</u> are in the bedroom.

   _________________________________________________

   b) I enjoyed hearing the laughter <u>of the children</u>.

   _________________________________________________

   c) We heard the shouts <u>of the people</u> from far away.

   _________________________________________________

# Possessive Nouns Review

Remember to use a **singular possessive noun** if **more than one thing** belongs to **one** person or thing.

*Examples:*   *the boy's shoes*  (two shoes belong to one boy)
        *the tree's roots*  (many roots belong to one tree)

Remember to use a **plural possessive noun** if **one thing** belongs to **more than one** person or thing.

*Examples:*   *the girls' secret*  (one secret belongs to several girls)
        *the frogs' croaking*  (one sound belongs to more than one frog)

**Circle** the correct **possessive noun** in each sentence.

a) Workers washed the ( building's  buildings' ) windows.
   (There is more than one building.)

b) The ( children's  childrens' ) father read a bedtime story.
   (There is more than one child.)

c) The ( student's  students' ) teacher was sick yesterday.
   (There is more than one student.)

d) A snow plow cleared the ( neighborhood's  neighborhoods' ) streets.
   (There is one neighborhood.)

e) The ( flower's  flowers' ) petals were brightly colored.
   (There is more than one flower.)

f) Corn grew tall in all the ( farmer's  farmers' ) fields.
   (There is one farmer.)

g) Mr. Chong came quickly when he heard the ( boy's  boys' ) shouts.
   (There is more than one boy.)

Remember to check your writing. Did you use singular and plural possessive nouns correctly?

# Nouns Review Quiz

1. Circle the **correct word** in brackets.

   a) A ( common  proper ) noun names a person, place, or thing that is not specific.

   b) A ( common  proper ) noun names a specific person, place, or thing.

   c) ( Common  Proper ) nouns always start with capital letters.

2. Add one **common noun** in each row. The common noun should fit the examples of proper nouns in the same row. The first row is completed for you.

| Common Nouns | Examples of Proper Nouns |
| --- | --- |
| a) *constellation* | *Little Dipper, Draco, Orion* |
| b) | *February, June, August* |
| c) | *Omaha, Colorado, West Virginia* |
| d) | *Europe, Australia, South America* |
| e) | *Mackenzie River, St. Lawrence River* |

3. Rewrite each sentence. Make the **proper nouns** start with **capital letters**.

   a) My dog fritzy chewed up saturn and mars from my solar system set.

   _______________________________________________

   b) The natural history museum in los angeles, has lots of dinosaur skeletons.

   _______________________________________________

   c) My brother troy built a model of the space shuttle *discovery* for science class.

4. In each sentence, circle the **plural noun** that is **spelled correctly**.

   a) Mitzi and Max blew out their birthday candles and made ( wishs  wishes ).

   b) Yu and Sam filled ( balloones  balloons ) with water to throw at each other.

   c) We swam at the nicest ( beaches  beachs ) on the west coast.

5. Write the **correct plural** for the noun in brackets. Careful! These are tricky.

   a) The _________________ made delicious foods for the mayor's party. (chef)

   b) The _________________ played on the climbing gym for hours. (child)

   c) Kerry stood all the books neatly on the _________________. (shelf)

   d) A big crowd of _______________ lined the parade route. (person)

   e) A large group of ___________ and _______________ sang in the choir. (man, woman)

6. Write the correct **singular** or **plural possessive noun** for the words in brackets.

   a) Sari gently brushed the ___________________. (hair of the dog)

   b) The ___________________ were hanging in the locker room. (gloves of the boxers)

   c) The ___________________ were bending the shelf. (contents of the box)

   d) Roger was excited to find out the ___________________. (secrets of the cave)

   e) The chair was ripped apart by the ___________________. (claws of the cats)

   f) ___________________ often match their dreams. (hopes of the people)

# Exploring Pronouns

A **pronoun** is a word that takes the place of a **noun**.
Use pronouns to avoid repeating the names of people and things in your writing.

Some pronouns take the place of **nouns that name people**.
These pronouns are *I*, *you*, *he*, *she*, *we*, *they*, *him*, *her*, *them*, *me*, and *us*.

Some pronouns take the place of **nouns that name things**.
These pronouns are *it*, *they*, and *them*.

Complete each sentence with the **correct pronoun**. The pronoun takes the place of the word or words in brackets.

a) ___________ is one of the fastest swimmers on our team. (Marie)

b) ___________ went for a walk on a warm spring day. (Raj and I)

c) My name is Mona. ___________ found the book you lost. (Mona)

d) Hi, Alex. Did ___________ finish your homework last night? (Alex)

e) Did she ask ___________ to water the plants? (the children)

f) ___________ love to play in the backyard. (the puppies)

g) Please give ___________ to Christina. (the muffin)

h) I put ___________ on the bottom shelf. (the books)

i) We did not see ___________ yesterday. (Mrs. Altman)

j) My name is Kevin. You can give the box to ___________. (Kevin)

k) Michelle invited ___________ to her birthday party. (you and me)

# Should You Use *I* or *Me*?

*I* and **me** are both pronouns that you can use to replace your own name. Sometimes, you might not be sure which pronoun to use in sentences like the ones below.

*Karen and ____ went to the store.* (Use *I* or **me**?)
*Ricardo waved to Cindy and ____.* (Use *I* or **me**?)

---

Here is one way to decide whether to use *I* or **me**:

**Step 1**
Take out of the sentence the other person or people who come **right before** the word **and**. Then take out the word **and**. It should be easier to decide which pronoun to use in the new sentence.

Original sentence: ~~Karen and~~ ____ *went to the store.*
New sentence: ____ *went to the store.* (Use *I* or **me**?)
New sentence with pronoun: *I went to the store.*

**Step 2**
In the original sentence, use the same pronoun you used in the new sentence.

*Karen and **I** went to the store.*

---

Here is another example:

*Ricardo waved to Cindy and ____.*

**Step 1**
Original sentence: *Ricardo waved to ~~Cindy and~~ ____.*
New sentence: *Ricardo waved to ____.* (Use *I* or **me**?)
New sentence with pronoun: *Ricardo waved to **me**.*

**Step 2**
*Ricardo waved to Cindy and **me**.*

1. In the first sentence, cross out words and write the **pronoun** (*I* or *me*) that works in the new sentence. Then write the original sentence with the **correct pronoun**.

   *Example:*

   ~~You and~~ __I__ *can play the game later.*
   *You and **I** can play the game later.*

   a) Luke and _______ sang two songs.

   _______________________________________________

   b) Mom gave the apples to Kylie and _______.

   _______________________________________________

   c) He said that Mario and _______ worked hard.

   _______________________________________________

   d) Dad asked Tamika and _______ to help.

   _______________________________________________

   e) Mom bought Julio and _________ a new video game.

   _______________________________________________

   f) I wonder if you and _________ will be famous.

   _______________________________________________

   g) The magician let Cindy and _________ help him.

   _______________________________________________

2. Fill in the blank with either **me** or **I**.

a) _______ like you.

b) You like _______.

c) You and _______ talked about our math homework.

d) I heard our math teacher talking about you and _______.

e) _______ wanted to buy some bubble gum.

f) Do you want to go to the movies with _______?

g) Jack says _______ have a cute cat.

h) Tessa is going to the library with _______ today.

i) _______ will study for the test with Marco tonight.

j) Kelly asked if _______ wanted to ride bikes on Saturday.

3. Write two sentences using the pronoun *I*.

______________________________________________

______________________________________________

4. Write two sentences using the pronoun **me**.

______________________________________________

______________________________________________

# Pronoun–Verb Agreement

The **subject** of an action verb is the person or thing doing the action. In the examples below, the subject is in bold and the action verb is underlined.

Examples: **Carlos** <u>fishes</u> in the lake on weekends.
The **turtle** slowly <u>crawls</u> across the log.
Three **birds** <u>perch</u> on the telephone wires.

The subject of the verb in each sentence above can be replaced by a pronoun. The pronoun becomes the subject of the verb.

Examples: **He** <u>fishes</u> in the lake on weekends.
**It** slowly <u>crawls</u> across the log.
**They** <u>perch</u> on the telephone wires.

When you use a pronoun as the subject of a verb in the present tense, make sure you use the correct form of the verb.

For most action verbs, add **s** to the present tense if the subject is the pronoun **he**, **she**, or **it**. **Do not** add **s** if the subject is **I**, **we**, **you**, or **they**. Look at the examples below.

| **Add *s*** | **Do Not Add *s*** |
| --- | --- |
| **She** <u>hears</u> the phone ring. | **I** <u>hear</u> the phone ring. |
| **He** <u>runs</u> down for the bus. | **We** <u>run</u> for the bus. |
| **It** <u>falls</u> in the mud. | **They** <u>fall</u> in the mud. |
| **She** quickly <u>opens</u> the curtains. | **You** quickly <u>open</u> the curtains. |

For most action verbs that end with **s**, **sh**, **ch**, or **x**, add **es** if the subject is the pronoun **he**, **she**, or **it**.

Example: **She** <u>presses</u> the elevator button.

When you use the correct form of the verb with a pronoun, we say that the pronoun and verb "agree."

Note that the verb **have** does not follow the rule of adding **s** when the subject is **he**, **she**, or **it**. This verb has special forms for the present tense.

Examples: **I** <u>have</u> two teeth missing.
**You** <u>have</u> three good friends.
**He** <u>has</u> a new skateboard.
**She** <u>has</u> a new kitten.

**You** all <u>have</u> some chores to do.
**We** <u>have</u> gifts for Grandma.
**They** <u>have</u> fresh bread to go with dinner.

# Pronoun–Verb Agreement (continued)

1. Circle the correct **verb** in brackets. Make sure that the **pronoun** and **verb** agree.

   a) He ( write  writes ) in his math notebook.

   b) They ( has  have ) a flock of chickens in their backyard.

   c) She ( wash  washes ) the dishes every night after dinner.

   d) We ( imagine  imagines ) how beautiful the mountains will be.

   e) It ( creep  creeps ) along the window ledge outside.

   f) I never ( space  spaces ) the candy hearts out evenly.

   g) You ( has  have ) beautiful hair and it ( curl  curls ) by itself.

   h) He ( want  wants ) to be an astronaut when he ( grow  grows ) up.

   i) I ( see  sees ) she ( has  have ) a new bicycle and it ( is  are ) blue.

2. Write the correct form of the **verb** in brackets to make the **pronoun** and **verb** agree.

   a) He ______________ a broken arm. (have)

   b) They ______________ to the top of the valley this afternoon. (hikes)

   c) We ______________ to my grandparents' house tomorrow. (travels)

   d) She ______________ homemade bread every Saturday. (make)

   e) I ______________ to see the movie, but I have no money. (wants)

   f) It is so cold outside, it ______________ like winter. (feel)

   g) You carefully ______________ up to the tree to peek at the bird. (creep)

   h) They ______________ together with their mother. (snuggles)

   i) She ______________ the curtains open to let the sunshine in. (leave)

# Possessive Pronouns

A **possessive pronoun** is a pronoun that shows **ownership.** Use the possessive pronouns below to show ownership.

**mine   yours   his   hers   ours   theirs   its**

*Examples: That book is <u>my book</u>. That book is **mine**.*
*The yellow scarf <u>belongs to Mary</u>. The yellow scarf is **hers**.*

Possessive pronouns **do not** use an **apostrophe** to show ownership.

Use **possessive pronouns** to complete the sentences.

a) I will clean my room, and you will clean <u>your room</u>.

   I will clean my room, and you will clean _____________.

b) The red car <u>belongs to Mr. and Mrs. Garcia.</u>

   The red car is _____________.

c) This shirt is missing one of the buttons <u>of the shirt</u>.

   This shirt is missing one of _____________ buttons.

d) This hamster <u>belongs to my sister and me</u>.

   This hamster is _____________.

e) I thought these were <u>his baseballs</u>, but they <u>belong to the girls</u>.

   I thought these were ___________, but they are ___________.

f) Does this book <u>belong to me</u>, or does it <u>belong to Tina</u>?

   Is this book ___________ or _____________?

# Exploring Possessive Pronouns

1. Fill in the blank with the correct **possessive pronoun**. The first one is done for you.

    a) I have a bike and a skateboard. The bike and skateboard are <u>mine</u>.

    b) I have a grape Popsicle and you have a cherry Popsicle. The grape Popsicle is

        ________. The cherry Popsicle is ________.

    c) My brother and I have a trampoline in the backyard. The trampoline is ________.

    d) My mom has a blue car. My dad has a black car. The blue car is ________. The

      black car is ________.

    e) My grandparents live in the apartment across the hall from us. The apartment is

      ________.

2. Draw a line from the **possessive pronouns** to the noun or pronoun they replace.

| | |
|---|---|
| a) mine | Jonathan |
| b) yours | Nina and I |
| c) his | I |
| d) hers | Monica and Abdul |
| e) ours | horse |
| f) theirs | you |
| g) its | Samantha |

3. Write a sentence using each **possessive pronoun** correctly.

a) mine

_______________________________________________

b) ours

_______________________________________________

c) yours

_______________________________________________

d) theirs

_______________________________________________

e) his

_______________________________________________

f) its

_______________________________________________

g) hers

_______________________________________________

4. Read the sentence carefully. Circle the correct **possessive pronoun** in brackets.

a) I wore my new running shoes yesterday. Mandy wore ( hers  theirs ) today.

b) That dog has hurt ( its  his ) paw on the stones.

c) Many people I know carry ( their  your ) cell phones everywhere.

d) On Friday, ( our  their ) cousins are coming to visit us.

e) Our maple tree is taller than ( theirs  its ).

# Pronouns Review Quiz

1. Complete each sentence with the **correct pronoun**. The pronoun takes the place of the word or words in brackets.

   a)  Amad and Ravi, I would like to invite _______ to come to my party. (Amad and Ravi)

   b) I asked Lu to walk to the library with ______. (I)

   c) Tim's baby sister loves to watch the puppy play. It makes ______ laugh. (baby sister)

   d) Lake Morey freezes in winter. Lots of people skate on _______. (Lake Morey)

   e) Ten birds are on my bird feeder. There is enough food for _______. (ten birds)

   f) Aunt Maya is coming to visit. _______ is bringing her new puppy. (Aunt Maya)

   g) Han and I met Jack at recess. ______ played catch with ________. (Han and I; Jack)

   h) My parents take good care of me and my sister. _______ love ______.
      (My parents; me and my sister)

   i) My best friend Sven has a bad cold. ______ hope ____ gets better soon. (Me; Sven)

2. Cross out the **other person or people** in the sentence. Decide whether to use *I* or *me*.

   a) The winning project in the science fair was created by Kenji, Tara, and ______.

   b) Maria, Jenny, and _______ had curled hair for the dance.

   c) Yesterday, two ants crawled all over the cat and _______.

   d) My dad and _______ mowed the lawn this afternoon.

   e) A butterfly landed on the chair where Larry and _____ sat.

   f) Mosquitos bit Mom, Dad, and _______ in the park this morning.

   g) Mrs. Ross asked whether you and _______ could take care of their kitten.

   h) Uncle Ted came to the zoo with my parents, my brother, and _________ today.

3. Circle the correct form of the **verb** in brackets to make the **pronoun** and **verb** agree.

a) You always ( wishes  wish ) me a happy birthday before anyone else.

b) They will ( make  makes ) two batches of cookies for the bake sale tomorrow.

c) I saw our new neighbor today. She ( have  has ) lots of plants for her new garden.

d) Our dog is very dirty. He ( roll  rolls ) in the mud whenever he gets a chance.

e) Every morning when I get up, I ( brush  brushes ) my hair.

f) That movie made me ( laughs  laugh ) until my sides hurt.

g) My mother told me we ( has  have ) a new baby coming soon.

h) Grandpa helped us ( paint  paints ) the bird house.

4. Rewrite each sentence. Use a **possessive pronoun** to replace the underlined words.

a) My hair is curly, and <u>your hair</u> is straight.

_______________________________________________

b) The boy left school without the jacket <u>that belongs to the boy</u>.

_______________________________________________

c) Bessie the cow could not find <u>the baby of Bessie</u> anywhere.

_______________________________________________

d) This week, the Brownies sold lots of <u>cookies that belong to the Brownies</u>.

_______________________________________________

# What Is an Adjective?

An **adjective** is a word that describes a noun.

*A huge bear came out of the woods.*

The word *huge* is an adjective that describes the noun *bear*.

1. Circle the **adjective** in each sentence. Underline the **noun** the adjective describes. Draw an arrow from the **adjective** to the **noun it describes**.

   *Example: The (loud) thunderstorm scared my puppy.*

   a) We wanted to explore the ancient castle.

   b) I watched a funny movie before I went to bed.

   c) The noisy children played on the slide in the park.

   d) Do not sit in the wobbly chair by the fireplace.

   e) Does the striped sweater still fit me?

2. Circle all the **adjectives** in each sentence. Underline the **noun** each adjective describes. Draw an arrow from each **adjective** to the **noun it describes**.

   a) Use warm water to wash the dirty floor.

   b) I wear the red coat on cold days in winter.

   c) An old truck drove down the bumpy road on a foggy night.

   d) A hungry lion was hiding in the tall grass.

   e) The sneaky thieves stole valuable jewels from the rich woman.

   f) The brave astronauts traveled in a fast spaceship.

   g) The tiny fish swam in the large aquarium.

# Using the Articles *A*, *An*, and *The*

The words *a*, *an*, and *the* are called **articles**. Use *a* before a **singular noun** that starts with a **consonant**. Use *an* before a **singular noun** that starts with a **vowel**. Look at the examples below.

*a* giraffe    *a* rainbow    *a* wish
*an* idea    *an* apple    *an* ocean

Use *the* before a **singular** or **plural noun**.

*the* piano    *the* umbrella    *the* clouds    *the* erasers

## Choosing Between *A* or *An* and *The*

Use *the* when you are talking about something **specific**. A specific thing is **one particular example**.

*__The__ dog on our front lawn does not belong to us.*

This sentence is not about just any dog. It is about one particular example of a dog— the dog that is on the writer's front lawn. The writer used *the* to talk about a **specific** dog.

A **specific** example can include **more than one** thing.

*__The__ butterflies I saw in the garden this morning were beautiful.*

This sentence is not about just any butterflies. It is about the particular butterflies the writer saw in the garden. The writer used *the* to talk about a **specific** example of a group of butterflies.

Use *a* or *an* when you are talking about something **in general**. That means you are **not** talking about a **specific** example.

*Dad took me to the mall to get __a coat__.*

The writer is talking about a coat **in general**. There is **not** one specific example of a coat that the writer has already seen and has decided to get.

*Dad took me to the mall to get __the coat__ we saw last week.*

This sentence is about **one particular example** of a coat, so the writer used *the* instead of *a*.

Sometimes, a **singular noun** has an **adjective** in front of it. If the sentence is **not** talking about a **specific** example and the adjective starts with a **vowel**, use *an*.

*Examples:* **an** *old attic*   **an** *easy question*   **an** *icy sidewalk*

If the **singular noun** is **not** a specific example and the **adjective** starts with a **consonant**, use *a*.

*Examples:* **a** *huge elephant*   **a** *red apple*   **a** *deep ocean*

1. Write the **correct word** (*a, an,* or *the*) in each sentence. Think about whether the sentence is about something **specific** or something **general**.

a) _________ tall maple tree in the backyard is 18 years old.

b) Mom wants to get _________ maple tree to plant in the backyard.

c) Whenever I get _________ idea, I write it down.

d) _________ idea that Kesha just explained sounds as though it might work.

e) _________ sweater with blue stripes was a gift from my grandparents.

f) All of _________ sweaters on this table are on sale.

g) Please raise your hand if you would like to ask _________ question.

h) Who knows _________ answer to the first question on the test?

i) My grandparents are looking for _________ apartment with a balcony.

j) I would like to find _________ interesting book about airplanes.

k) Mom would like to get _________ orange tablecloth.

l) Darnell hoped to find _________ long earthworm in the garden.

m) Anna didn't see _________ green umbrella in any of the stores.

# Adjectives Before and After Nouns

Sometimes an adjective comes **before** the noun it describes.
Sometimes an adjective comes **after** the noun it describes.

**Before a noun:** *The pink roses are beautiful.*

**After a noun:** *The roses are pink.*

1. Underline the adjective in the sentence. Circle whether the adjective is **before** or **after** the noun.

   a) Do you think the baby is cute?   *before   after*

   b) The women were tired after playing hockey.   *before   after*

   c) The wild horse galloped across the field.   *before   after*

   d) He made sandwiches because the children were hungry.   *before   after*

   e) Did the doctor look at your sore throat?   *before   after*

   f) Remember to recycle the empty jars.   *before   after*

2. Look for **more than one** adjective in each sentence below. Circle each **adjective** and underline each **noun**. Draw an arrow from each **adjective** to the **noun it describes**.

   a) The young magician did tricks that were amazing.

   b) The fresh muffins are delicious.

   c) The movie was long and boring.

   d) Orange and yellow leaves fell from the old tree.

   e) Our new teacher has red hair that is long and curly.

   f) My nephew Ben is an amazing skier.

# Adjectives Can Describe How Many

An **adjective** describes a noun. Some adjectives answer the question "How many?" **Numbers** can be adjectives.

*Example: Mr. Tanaka has* four *children.*

Some adjectives answer the question "How many?" but they do not describe exactly how many.

*Example: She has* several *books about dinosaurs.*

**Several** is an adjective that describes the noun **books**. **Several** does not tell exactly how many books, but it tells us she has more than one.

---

1. Underline the **adjective** in the sentence. Circle whether the adjective **does** or **does not** tell **exactly how many**.

   a) Four students were sick with the flu.      *does      does not*

   b) Mr. Mills picked some tomatoes from his garden.      *does      does not*

   c) Few people wanted to go to the concert.      *does      does not*

   d) Sandra found several fossils by the ocean.      *does      does not*

   e) We saw three robins and many sparrows in the trees.      *does      does not*

   f) All children should learn to read and write.      *does      does not*

2. Circle all the **adjectives** and underline all the **nouns**. Draw an arrow from each **adjective** to the **noun it describes**.

   a) The old house has several windows that are broken.

   b) Do all butterflies have colorful wings?

   c) Many parents have some questions for the new principal.

   d) The eager students have a limited time to finish their quiz.

# Using Adjectives to Compare Two Things

You can use an **adjective** to **compare two things**.

*Example: The house is <u>tall</u>, but the tree is <u>taller</u>.*

**Tall** and **taller** are adjectives. **Taller** is an adjective that compares two things. This sentence **compares** how tall the house and the tree are.

For many adjectives that have **one syllable**, just add *er* to make an adjective that compares two things.

*Examples:  short – shorter    bright – brighter*

1. Complete each sentence. Change the **adjective** in brackets to make it **compare two things**.

   a) A cheetah runs _______________ than a tiger. (fast)

   b) This story is _______________ than the last one I wrote. (long)

   c) Your mattress is _______________ than my mattress. (soft)

   d) The smoke detector is _______________ than my alarm clock. (loud)

   e) The girls walked _______________ than usual, so it took longer to get to park. (slow)

   f) The lemonade tasted _______________ with more sugar. (sweet)

   g) Joe is _______________ than his brother. (tall)

   h) Today feels _______________ than yesterday. (cool)

   i) Elise is _______________ than her sister. (young)

   j) My bedroom is _______________ than your  bedroom. (clean)

   k) This stone is _______________ than that stone. (rough)

# Using Adjectives to Compare Two Things (continued)

2. For the adjectives in brackets, double the **final consonant** before adding *er*.

*Examples: hot – hotter    big – bigger    thin – thinner    fat – fatter    sad – sadder*

a) His marker is _______________ than her marker. (thin)

b) Today is _______________ than yesterday. (hot)

c) My hair is _______________ than my brother's hair. (red)

d) The new suitcase is _______________ than the old suitcase. (big)

e) When we came in from the rain, I was _______________ than my dog. (wet)

f) The little boy was _______________ than his sister. (sad)

g) My cake turned out much _______________ than I expected. (flat)

h) She exercises and runs every day. She is _______________ than most people. (fit)

3. Change the **adjective** in the brackets to make it **compare two things**. Watch out for **final consonants** that need to be **doubled**.

a) That red rock is _______________ than this gray rock. (round)

b) The book you are reading is much _______________ than the book I am reading. (slim)

c) My brother is 6 years _______________ than my sister. (old)

d) The lightbulb in that lamp is _______________ than the lightbulb in this lamp. (dim)

e) I studied _______________ for tomorrow's science test than I ever have before. (hard)

f) That puppy is _______________ than the other puppies. (fat)

g) My brother kept teasing me until I got _______________ than ever before. (mad)

# Adjectives to Compare More Than Two Things

You can use an adjective to compare **more than two things**.

*Example: Pat was the fastest runner in the race.*

**Fastest** is an adjective. This sentence **compares** all the runners in the race. Pat was the fastest of all the runners.

For most adjectives that have one syllable, add **est** to make an adjective that compares more than two things.

*Example: cold – coldest*

1. Use the correct form of the adjective in brackets to **compare more than two things.** Then tell what is being compared in each sentence.

   a) This knife is the _________________ knife in the drawer. (sharp)

   This sentence compares all the _______________________________.

   b) My sister is the _________________ child in my family. (young)

   This sentence compares all the _______________________________.

   c) Rico is the _________________ student in his class. (tall)

   This sentence compares _______________________________.

   d) My closet is the _________________ in the house. (clean)

   This sentence compares all the _______________________________.

   e) Amy's frog was the _________________ frog in the race. (fast)

   This sentence compares all the _______________________________.

   f) Teddy the horse is the _________________ animal on my uncle's farm. (old)

   This sentence compares all the _______________________________.

2. For the adjectives in brackets, double the **final consonant** before adding *est*.

*Examples: hot – hottest   big – biggest   thin – thinnest   fat – fattest   sad – saddest*

a) We bought the _________________ tent in the store. (big)

This sentence compares _________________________________________.

b) That is the _________________ movie I have ever seen. (sad)

This sentence compares _________________________________________.

c) I took the _________________ cookie on the plate. (thin)

This sentence compares _________________________________________.

d) My pillow is so old, it is the _________________ pillow in the house. (flat)

This sentence compares _________________________________________.

e) Last week was the _________________ week of the summer so far. (hot)

This sentence compares _________________________________________.

f) My brother's car is the _________________ car I have ever seen. (red)

This sentence compares _________________________________________.

g) After the water balloon fight, Tia was the _________________ of all the kids. (wet)

This sentence compares _________________________________________.

h) Brown dwarf stars are the _________________ stars in the known universe. (dim)

This sentence compares _________________________________________.

# More Adjectives That Compare

Make sure you use the correct form of these adjectives that compare.

| Adjective | To Compare Two Things | To Compare More Than Two Things |
|---|---|---|
| good | better | best |
| bad | worse | worst |
| far | farther | farthest |
| many | more | most |

Use the correct form of the **adjectives** in brackets. Write *the* before an adjective that compares **more than two things**.

a) The movie about robots was _______________________ than the movie about buried treasure. (good)

b) Of all the students in my class, Sanjay has _______________________ pets. (many)

c) Ken's house is _______________________ from school than my house. (far)

d) This storm is _______________________ storm we have had all winter. (bad)

e) Eva has many baseball cards, but I have _______________________. (many)

f) Max has a bad cold, but Kate's cold is _______________________. (bad)

g) This restaurant is _______________________ restaurant in town. (good)

h) Miguel and Elizabeth both live far from me, but Miguel's house is

_______________________ from my house. (far)

# Spelling Adjectives That Compare

Make sure you use the correct spelling for **adjectives that compare**.

|  | To Compare Two Things | To Compare More Than Two Things |
|---|---|---|
| Adjectives that end with *e*<br>*Example: large* | Add *r*<br>*larger* | Add *st*<br>*largest* |
| Adjectives that end with a **consonant + y**<br>*Example: silly* | Change the *y* to *i* and add *er*<br>*sillier* | Change the *y* to *i* and add *est*<br>*silliest* |

Remember to double the final consonant of these adjectives before you add *er* or *est*:

**hot   big   thin   fat   flat   sad**

Decide whether each sentence compares **two things** or more than **two things.** Then write the correct form of the adjective in brackets.

a) This is the _________________ road in the city. (bumpy)

b) The red apple is _________________ than the green apple. (ripe)

c) That is the _________________ picture you have ever painted. (pretty)

d) The white kitten is _________________ than the black kitten. (cute)

e) She is the _________________ person I have ever met. (wise)

f) Tomorrow will be a _________________ day than today. (sunny)

g) The black puppy is _________________ than the brown puppy. (fat)

h) This pancake is the _________________ pancake on the plate. (thin)

i) Main Street is _________________ than Maple Street. (flat)

j) My bedroom is the _________________ room in the house. (messy)

# Adjectives and Articles Review Quiz

1. Circle all the **adjectives**. Draw an arrow from each **adjective** to the **noun** it describes.

   a) My muddy boots left dirty footprints all over the clean floor.

   b) Tammy's dog has puppies, and all of them are different colors.

   c) We made blueberry pancakes for our family brunch on Sunday.

   d) On Thursdays, we play music for the elderly people at the seniors' home.

2. Use *a*, *an*, or *the*. Read the sentence to check if it talks about something **specific**.

   a) I heard _______ squirrel chattering loudly in the backyard.

   b) Mrs. Mitchell says she likes _______ flowers my mother planted on the weekend.

   c) My cousin Lee says she wants to see _______ elephant at _______ zoo today.

   d) _______ principal called everyone into _____ auditorium to make _____ announcement.

3. Underline the **adjective**. Circle whether the adjective comes **before** or **after** the noun it describes.

   a) The striped snake slithered quickly across the path.   *before   after*

   b) The stripes on the notebook were blue and purple.   *before   after*

   c) The cake my brother and I made was messy, but delicious.   *before   after*

   d) My class wrote a long and difficult quiz on Friday.   *before   after*

4. Underline the **adjective** in the sentence. Circle whether the adjective **does** or **does not** tell **exactly how many**.

   a) Many acorns are forgotten after squirrels bury them.   *does   does not*

   b) That boy kicked five goals into the net at soccer practice today.   *does   does not*

   c) Our dog needed several baths after a skunk sprayed him.   *does   does not*

   d) Four people called about the car my father is selling.   *does   does not*

5. Use the correct form of the **adjective** in brackets to **compare two things**. Double the last **consonant** when necessary.

   a) I can run fast, but my friend Tony can run a lot _____________________. (fast)

   b) My brother and I got caught in a rain storm and we are the _________________ we have ever been. (wet)

   c) Mike is a good singer, but Ali is __________________. (good)

   d) Your necklace is much ____________ than my necklace. (long)

   e) Their driveway is a lot _______________ than our driveway. (flat)

6. Use the correct form of the adjective in brackets to **compare more than two things**. Remember to write *the* when needed.

   a) This Monday has been _____________________ day of the winter so far. (cold)

   b) Joe is ___________________ math student in the whole school. (good)

   c) Jamal can jump __________________ of all the boys on the basketball team. (high)

   d) The three-toed sloth is _____________________ animal in the world. (slow)

7. Use the adjective in brackets to **compare two things or more than two things**. Use the correct spelling and *the* when needed.

   a) Our kittens are all fluffy, but this kitten is ____________________. (fluffy)

   b) Yu's dog was _______________ at the dog show. (large)

   c) That maple tree is _____________________ tree in the neighborhood. (shady)

   d) This yellow banana is _______________ than that green banana. (ripe)

   e) The tornado damage was _______________ ever in that province. (bad)

# Action Verbs

The **subject** of a sentence is the person or thing that the sentence is about.

An **action verb** is a word that tells what the subject does or did. In the examples below, the subject is underlined and the action verb is in bold.

*Example: <u>My sister</u> **paints** her fingernails.*
In this sentence, the verb *paints* tells what the subject (*my sister*) does.

*Example: <u>A large cat</u> **walked** up our driveway.*
In this sentence, the verb *walked* tells what the subject (*a large cat*) did.

The verbs *paints* and *walked* both express action, so these verbs are action verbs.

Underline the **action verb** in the sentence. **Do not** underline verbs that **do not** express an action.

a) Her whole family attended the concert.

b) She eats cereal for breakfast.

c) The waiter wiped the table clean.

d) His uncle is a custodian at the school.

e) The sound of laughter echoes throughout the auditorium.

f) The paper went into the recycle bin.

g) The baby giggled at the funny face.

h) New plants grew in the garden.

i) Andrew skis fast down the mountain.

j) Mom told us about the surprise.

k) My grandfather fixed my bike.

l) The detective searches for clues.

# Linking Verbs

A **linking verb** is a verb that does **not** show an action.

Look at the verbs in the sentences below. Notice that these verbs do **not** show an **action** that someone did or is doing.

*Examples: The day **was** cold and gray.*
*Jason **feels** sick this morning.*
*Mr. Dupuis **is** a firefighter.*

The verbs in the sentences above are all linking verbs.

---

## What does a linking verb do if it doesn't show action?

**1.** A linking verb can link the **subject** of the sentence (the person or thing the sentence is about) to an adjective that describes the subject.

*Example: The day **was** cold and gray.*

The subject of the sentence is the noun *day*. The adjectives *cold* and *gray* describe the subject. The linking verb *was* links the subject to the adjectives that describe it.

*Example: Jason **feels** sick this morning.*

The subject of the sentence is the proper noun *Jason*. The adjective *sick* describes the subject. The linking verb *feels* links the subject to the adjective that describes it.

**2.** A linking verb can link the **subject** of the sentence to a noun that is another name for the subject.

*Example: Mr. Dupuis **is** a firefighter.*

The subject of the sentence is the proper noun *Mr. Dupuis*. The noun *firefighter* is another name for the subject. The linking verb *is* links the subject to a noun that is another name for the subject. So *Mr. Dupuis* and *firefighter* are two nouns that name the same person.

1. The **subject** in each sentence is underlined. The **linking verb** is in bold. Circle the **adjective** that describes the subject **or** the **noun** that is another name for the subject. Then circle the **correct answer** in the next sentence.

   a) <u>Shonda</u> **was** excited about the sleepover.
   The linking verb connects the subject to ( an adjective   a noun ).

   b) My <u>dog</u> **seems** scared of something.
   The linking verb connects the subject to ( an adjective   a noun ).

   c) His <u>sister</u> **is** a cashier at the building supply store.
   The linking verb connects the subject to ( an adjective   a noun ).

   d) The <u>crowd</u> **became** restless halfway through his speech.
   The linking verb connects the subject to ( an adjective   a noun ).

   e) My <u>grandfather</u> **was** a veteran of World War II.
   The linking verb connects the subject to ( an adjective   a noun ).

2. Underline the **linking verb** in each sentence.

   a) Jessie doesn't feel nervous about her speech.

   b) Mom's roasted chicken dinner tastes delicious.

   c) Karen and I became good friends thirty years ago.

   d) Mr. Walter is my next door neighbor.

   e) The music sounds like church bells.

   f) That boy in the green T-shirt looks a lot like the boy in the striped shirt.

   g) That thunder clap was really loud!

   h) Those roses stay beautiful for a long time.

# Exploring Present Tense Verbs

A **verb** is word that tells what someone or something is doing.

Use **present tense verbs** to name an action that is **happening now**.

Change the spelling of verbs when **he, she,** or **it** is the subject of the sentence and **he, she,** or **it** is doing the action.

**One Person or Thing**
*I fall*
*You fall*
*He/She/It* **falls**

**More Than One Person or Thing**
*We fall*
*You fall*
*They fall*

1. Circle the correct **present tense** of the verb in brackets.

   a) I ( return  returns ) the books to the library.

   b) My dog ( wait  waits ) for me to come home.

   c) The microwave ( heat  heats ) food quickly.

   d) We ( climb  climbs ) the stairs to the second floor.

2. Look at the verb in each sentence. Choose the word in brackets that **works with the verb**. Write the **correct word** to complete the sentence.

   a) _____________ takes the letters to the mailbox. (Mom   We)

   b) _____________ cook chicken on the barbecue. (She   They)

   c) _____________ whispers a secret to a friend. (You   Angelo)

   d) _____________ helps me with my homework.  (He   They)

3. Circle the word or words that **work with each verb**.

   a) ( Mom and Dad   Tracey ) waves goodbye to us.

   b) ( The kittens   The kitten ) play with the ball of yarn.

   c) ( The tree   The trees ) sways back and forth in the wind.

   d) ( The people  The woman ) take the train to Miami.

     

4. Fill in the blank with the correct **verb**.

a) I ___________ my lunch at 12:00 every day. (eat)

b) She ___________ very well. (dance)

c) Robert ___________ home from school at 3:30. (walk)

d) We ___________ soccer practice tonight. (have)

e) Mindy, Karl, and Sara ___________ the piano. (play)

f) Rani ___________ fruit salad for dinner tonight. (make)

g) Mario and Tony ___________ newspapers after school every day. (deliver)

5. Look at the nouns in brackets. Write the correct **noun** or **pronoun** that works with the verb.

a) ___________________ walks the dog every morning. (Cindy    We)

b) ___________________ make pizza on Fridays. (They    My dad)

c) ___________________ smiles at the neighbor. (Sam and Carl    Trisha)

d) ___________________ shoot hoops in the driveway. (My brother    My friends)

e) The ___________________ bounces very high. (basketball    basketballs)

f) ___________________ paints houses for a living. (My uncle    Sam and Dennis)

g) ___________________ walk dogs on weekends. (My sister    Kelly and Kim)

h) ___________________ explains math better than my teacher. (No one    My parents)

# Exploring Past Tense Verbs

**Past tense verbs** tell what happened in the **past.** Look at these examples:

| Verb | Present Tense | Past Tense |
|---|---|---|
| talk | Today, I talk. | Yesterday, I talked. |
| | Today, she talks. | Yesterday, she talked. |

For many verbs, add *ed* to the verb to make the past tense.
If the verb already ends with **e**, just add *d*.

1. Write these verbs in **past tense**.

a) talk ___________________

b) pour ___________________

c) walk ___________________

d) mix ___________________

e) play ___________________

f) fix ___________________

g) dance ___________________

h) create ___________________

i) smell ___________________

j) jump ___________________

2. Rewrite each sentence. Put the **underlined verb** in the **past tense**.

a) I <u>walk</u> to school with my friends.

___________________________________________________

b) I <u>fix</u> the mistakes I made on my homework.

___________________________________________________

c) My sister <u>plays</u> the fiddle at the competition.

___________________________________________________

3. Circle the **tense** used in each sentence.

a) I <u>created</u> a picture with paints and crayons.  *present tense   past tense*

b) My sister <u>poured</u> a glass of milk.  *present tense   past tense*

c) My friends and I <u>play</u> soccer on the weekends.  *present tense   past tense*

d) Manny and Julio talked about baseball for hours.  *present tense   past tense*

e) Amy said she reads an entire book every weekend.  *present tense   past tense*

f) The brave knight slayed the fierce dragon.  *present tense   past tense*

g) Seven noisy monkeys play in the treetops.  *present tense   past tense*

4. Write the **past tense** of the verb in brackets.

a) Tina ___________ her paper airplane, but it did not fly straight. (aim)

b) Sergio quickly _________________ nails into the roof shingles. (hammer)

c) The kind man _______________ the elderly woman across the street yesterday. (help)

d) The squirrel quickly _______________ it could not climb onto the bird feeder. (learn)

e) My uncle worked for a company that ___________ damaged ships. (repair)

f) The ice cream _______________ quickly in the summer heat. (melt)

g) The strong man _______________ a couch equal to his own weight. (lift)

# Tricky Past Tense Verbs

The **past tense** of some verbs does not end with **ed**. Watch out for these tricky verbs when you write in the past tense.

| Present Tense | Past Tense | Present Tense | Past Tense |
|---|---|---|---|
| buy, buys | bought | get, gets | got |
| come, comes | came | give, gives | gave |
| draw, draws | drew | go, goes | went |
| drink, drinks | drank | have, has | had |
| drive, drives | drove | know, knows | knew |
| eat, eats | ate | say, says | said |
| fall, falls | fell | take, takes | took |
| find, finds | found | think, thinks | thought |

Complete each sentence by writing the **past tense** of the verb in brackets.

a) My family ______________ to the beach in the summer. (drives)

b) My grandfather ________________ my brother and I gifts for our birthdays. (gives)

c) My brother ______________ to go to summer camp with me. (gets)

d) My teacher __________________ snacks every day at recess. (eats)

e) I ______________ home late from school when I _________ piano lessons.
   (come, have)

f) My puppy __________ down while playing catch. (falls)

g) You ______________ to finish your homework before playing video games. (have)

h) I ______________ hot chocolate after playing in the snow. (drink)

i) We __________________ turns playing video games. (take)

j) They ______________ to the mall to buy new shoes. (go)

# Exploring Future Tense Verbs

**Future tense verbs** tell about actions that will happen in the **future**. To make future tense verbs, use the helping verb **will** plus the verb in present tense.

**One Person or Thing**
*I will walk*
*You will walk*
*He/She/It will walk*

**More Than One Person or Thing**
*We will walk*
*You will walk*
*They will walk*

Use the helping verb **will** to put each sentence into future tense.

a) The babysitter _______________ when my parents go out for dinner. (comes)

b) My mom and I _______________ to the store to get cupcakes. (walk)

c) Jean-Paul _______________ hockey during the winter. (plays)

d) Liam _______________ cross-country in the fall. (runs)

e) Xavier, Sebastian, and Riley _______________ lots of books in the summer. (read)

f) They _______________ into the pool when it is hot and sunny. (jump)

g) I _______________ cereal and fruit for breakfast on the weekend. (eat)

h) My friends _______________ lemonade at my birthday party. (drink)

i) I _______________ my dad wash the dishes after dinner. (help)

j) We _______________ about gears and pulleys in science class. (learn)

k) My brother _______________ the water in the fish tank this weekend. (change)

l) Our grandparents _______________ to Florida this winter. (travel)

# Helping Verbs for Future Tense

Use **helping verbs** to make our meaning clear.

Helping verbs can tell us if something will happen in the future. The helping verb we use for future tense is **will**.

Other helping verbs tell us that something <u>might</u> happen.

*Examples:* **would**, **could**, **should**, **might**, **may**, and **can**.

Fill in the blank with the **helping verb** in brackets that fits best.

a) I ______________ have gone to the mall, if I were not grounded. (could    can)

b) My sister __________ do twelve laps in the swimming pool. (can    may)

c) You ______________ not eat cookies before dinner. (would    should)

d) My dad says I __________ go to the park to play with my friends. (would    may)

e) You ____________ do your homework before you play outside. (may    should)

f) "____________ Sally come out to play?" (Should    Could)

g) "___________I please go to the washroom, Mr. Smith?" (May    Can)

h) The glass __________ overflow if you do not turn off the tap soon. (might    should)

i) Carlos __________ have gone to the park with us, but he was sick. (would    can)

j) You _________ go see the monkeys when you visit the zoo. (would    should)

k) I can hear thunder, so there ____________ be a storm soon. (may  would)

l) Meghan ___________ touch her chin with her tongue. (could  can)

# Using *May, Might,* and *Must* as Helping Verbs

Use the helping verb *may* or *might* when you want to say that an action is **possible**, but you do not know for sure if it will happen.

*Examples: Roberto may visit us tomorrow. It might rain tonight.*

You can also use the helping verb *may* when someone is **asking for or giving permission**. *Examples: May I go? Yes, you may go.*

Use the helping verb *must* in these situations:

• You are saying something that you believe is **probably true**.
  *Example: She left school an hour ago, so she must be home by now.*

• You are saying that something is **required or necessary**.
  *Example: Students must leave the school when the fire alarm rings.*

Think about the idea in each sentence, and then circle the **correct word** in brackets. On the next line, circle the **reason for your answer**.

a) She eats an apple every day, so she ( may  must ) love apples.
   ( possible action   permission   probably true   required or necessary )

b) All cars ( might  must ) stop at a red light.
   ( possible action   permission   probably true   required or necessary )

c) Yes, you ( may  might ) borrow my red pen.
   ( possible action   permission   probably true   required or necessary )

d) I cannot find my key anywhere, so I ( may  must ) have lost it.
   ( possible action   permission   probably true   required or necessary )

e) She is feeling tired, so she ( might  must ) go to bed early.
   ( possible action   permission   probably true   required or necessary )

f) You ( may  must ) plug in the television before you can watch it.
   ( possible action   permission   probably true   required or necessary )

g) The sky is getting cloudy, so it ( may  must ) rain.
   ( possible action   permission   probably true   required or necessary )

# Using *Am*, *Is*, and *Are* as Helping Verbs

Use *am*, *is*, and *are* as helping verbs to show that an action is **still happening now**.

*Examples: I am sing**ing**. You are sing**ing**. He is sing**ing**. They are sing**ing**.*

Notice that when you use *am*, *is*, or *are* as a helping verb, you need to add *ing* to the **main verb**.

What you do if the verb in the sentence is *am*, *is*, or *are*?
Change the verb to *being* and use *am*, *is*, or *are* as a helping verb.

*Example: Lena is helpful. Lena is being helpful.*

Complete each sentence. Use a **helping verb** and the **verb in brackets** to show that the action is **still happening now**.

a) Mrs. Richards _____________________ her lawn. (mow)

b) The dogs _____________________ at the stranger. (bark)

c) The telephone _____________________. (ring)

d) You _____________________ very fast. (walk)

e) The leaves _____________________ from the trees. (fall)

f) The plumber _____________________ the leaky pipe. (fix)

g) I _____________________ to my favorite song. (listen)

h) The kitten _____________________ silly. (is)

i) The people _____________________ very noisy. (are)

j) I _____________________ careful with the sharp scissors. (am)

k) We _____________________ quiet while the teacher talks. (are)

# Using *Was* and *Were* as Helping Verbs

Use *was* and *were* as helping verbs to show that **one action was happening in the past** when **another action happened**.

*Example: I was washing the floor when the doorbell rang.*

Notice that when you use *was* or *were* as a helping verb, you need to add *ing* to the **main verb.**

1. Complete each sentence. Use a **helping verb** and the **verb in brackets** to show that the action **was happening when another action happened.**

   a) We ____________________ soccer when Carlos hurt his foot. (play)

   b) I ____________________ for my hat when Dad called me. (look)

   c) You ____________________ a book when I saw you. (read)

   d) They ____________________ a video when Sam sneezed. (watch)

   e) She ____________________ when the thunder woke her up. (sleep)

2. Join each pair of sentences. Make changes to show that the **second action** happened while the **first action** was happening.

   *Example: He painted the house. He fell off the ladder.*
   *He was painting the house when he fell off the ladder.*

   a) The man walked home. He slipped.

   ______________________________________________________

   b) Tina worked. Frank called her.

   ______________________________________________________

   c) I looked for my hat. You found it.

   ______________________________________________________

# Spelling Verbs That End with *ing*

Add *ing* to verbs when you are using these helping verbs:
*am   is   are   was   were*

For some verbs, you need to make spelling changes before you add *ing*.

**Verbs that end with a silent e**
Take off the silent **e** and add *ing*.      *Example: write – writing*

**Verbs that end with *ie***
Change *ie* to *y* and add *ing*.      *Example: lie – lying*

**One-syllable verbs that end with *consonant + vowel + consonant***
Double the final consonant and add *ing*.    *Example: hop – hopping*

**Do not** follow this rule if the verb ends with *w*, *x*, or *y*. Just add *ing*.
*Example: sew – sewing*

1. Add *ing* to each of the verbs.

a) give _______________________

b) divide _______________________

c) hope _______________________

d) invite _______________________

e) die _______________________

f) untie _______________________

g) run _______________________

h) sit _______________________

i) jog _______________________

j) row _______________________

k) fix _______________________

l) cut _______________________

m) say _______________________

n) win _______________________

2. Add *ing* to each of the verbs. Watch for verbs that need spelling changes.

a) ski _______________________

b) get _______________________

c) shake _______________________

d) enjoy _______________________

e) see _______________________

f) stop _______________________

# Verbs Review Quiz

1. Underline the **action verb** in each sentence. Some sentences have more than one verb. **Do not** underline verbs that **do not** express an action.

   a) The monkeys groomed each other on the tree branches.

   b) Squids swim backward to escape from danger.

   c) Jeff called and said he should arrive soon.

   d) Maya does not know that Zach is here.

2. Underline the **linking verb**. Circle *ADJ* if the linking verb connects the subject to **an adjective**. Circle *N* if the linking verb connects the subject to a **noun**.

   a) The air outside smells like rain.  *ADJ   N*

   b) Hundreds of gnats flying in big swarms are a bother in warm weather.  *ADJ   N*

   c) Cubes of colorful jello feel wonderful on my tongue.  *ADJ   N*

   d) That robin seems happy with her nest in our maple tree.  *ADJ   N*

3. Use the correct **present tense verb** for the verb in brackets.

   a) John _________________ books at the library. (read)

   b) My aunt's cat _________________ in the chair by the window. (sleep)

   c) The blue whale _______________ up the coast in the summer. (swim)

   d) The baby _________________ whenever the dog barks. (giggle)

   e) Zara _______________ my eraser in class every day. (borrow)

   f) My cousin _____________ in the deep end of the pool. (dive)

4. Read the sentence carefully. Circle the correct **past tense verb**.

   a) Jordan ( took   made ) a hippo out of clay in art class yesterday.

   b) Cassie ( helped  made ) her mother fold the laundry last weekend.

   c) The big owl ( scratched  sat ) in the tree watching for a mouse to pass by.

   d) The angry rattlesnake ( straightened  coiled ) up ready to strike.

5. Circle the **helping verb** in brackets that fits best.

   a) Today, Ravi ( will  might ) color a beautiful picture of a horse he drew in art class.

   b) It is very hot out today, so the sun ( could  must ) be out.

   c) My mom said I ( can  may ) go to Tao's house after school.

   d) The forms say I ( might  must ) sign my name on the dotted line.

6. Use *am*, *is*, or *are* and the verb in brackets to show the action **happening now**.

   a) Scotty _________________ for the quiz coming up on Wednesday. (study)

   b) All of my hamsters _____________________ their fur. (groom)

   c) I ___________________ shopping with my aunt today. (go)

   d) The tiniest ant _____________________ the biggest piece of food. (carry)

7. Use *was* or *were* with the **verb in brackets** to show that something **happened in the past**. Use the ending *ing*.

   a) Mr. Lucas _____________________ his garden when it started to rain. (water)

   b) Our neighbor's cats _____________________ along the top of our fence. (walk)

   c) Kim _____________________ about riding a pony. (dream)

   d) Dozens of ants _______________________ on the kitchen counter. (crawl)

# Adverbs That Describe How, Where, and When

An **adverb** is used to describe a verb or an action.

A word is being used as an adverb when you can answer **how, where,** or **when** an action happens.

Below is a list of some examples of different adverbs.

| How | Where | When |
|---|---|---|
| angrily | above | after |
| beautifully | anywhere | afternoon |
| boldly | away from | always |
| bravely | backward | before |
| calmly | behind | daily |
| carefully | below | early |
| cheerfully | beside | evening |
| clumsily | between | finally |
| eagerly | close by | first |
| easily | downstairs | frequently |
| eventually | east | hourly |
| foolishly | everywhere | late |
| gently | here | later |
| gladly | indoors | monthly |
| happily | inside | morning |
| honestly | nearby | never |
| impatiently | north | next |
| kindly | nowhere | now |
| lazily | outside | occasionally |
| loudly | somewhere | recently |
| mysteriously | south | sometimes |
| politely | there | soon |
| quickly | throughout | today |
| quietly | under | tomorrow |
| sadly | underground | tonight |
| slowly | upstairs | usually |
| swiftly | west | weekend |
| wisely | worldwide | yesterday |

# Some Adverbs Describe How

An **adverb** describes a **verb**. Some adverbs describe **how** an action happens. Look at the example below.

*Walter quickly tied his shoelaces.*
The adverb **quickly** tells **how** Walter tied his shoelaces.

Sometimes an adverb comes **after** the verb it describes.

*Sheila sang beautifully*

1. In each sentence, circle the adverb that describes **how an action happens**. Underline the verb that the **adverb describes**. Draw an arrow from the adverb to the **verb it describes**.

   a) I spoke loudly so everyone could hear.

   b) The bird flew swiftly to the top of a tree.

   c) Mr. Kato gently rocks the sleeping baby.

   d) Tara carefully checked her homework.

   e) We were lost, so we politely asked for directions.

   f) Ralph writes his name neatly at the top of the page.

   g) The woman shouted angrily at the barking dogs.

   h) The package mysteriously vanished.

2. Look for and circle more than one adverb that describes **how** in the sentences below.

   a) Suddenly the clouds disappeared, and the sun shone brightly.

   b) Slowly and silently, the thief tiptoed from room to room.

   c) The man spoke softly and calmly as he told us what had happened.

# Some Adverbs Describe When

An **adverb** describes a **verb**. Some adverbs describe **when** an action happens.

*Example: David washed his hair today.*
The adverb **today** describes **when** David washed his hair.

Some adverbs describe **when** an action happens, but they **do not** describe **exactly when** it happens.

*Example: Nancy came later.*
The adverb **later** describes **when** Nancy came.

Some adverbs describe **when** by telling the **order of events**.

*Example: Jacob threw the ball first.*

In each sentence, circle the adverb that tells **when** an action happens. Underline the **verb the adverb describes**. (You do not need to underline any helping verbs.) Draw an arrow from the adverb to the **verb it describes**.

a) We will watch an interesting video tonight.

b) Can the children by the pool swim now?

c) Yesterday, we wrapped the gifts for our cousins.

d) The train from Chicago arrived late.

e) Soon all this snow will melt.

f) It is wise to drink water frequently when the temperature is hot.

g) Tony finished the race last.

h) Next, Gabriela will read her story.

i) Please call me before you come over.

# Some Adverbs Describe Where

An **adverb** describes a **verb**. Some adverbs describe **where** an action happens.

*Example: The boys played upstairs*
The adverb **upstairs** describes **where** the boys played.

Some adverbs describe **where** an action happens, but they **do not** describe **exactly** **where** it happens.

*Example: She left her scarf somewhere*
The adverb **somewhere** describes **where** she left her scarf, but it does not describe an exact place.

1. In each sentence, circle the adverb that tells **where** an action happens. Underline the **verb the adverb describes**. Draw an arrow from the adverb to the **verb it describes**.

   a) Please hang your coats here.

   b) He found a post office nearby.

   c) I looked everywhere for the lost library book.

   d) We took the boxes downstairs.

   e) Put your books anywhere.

   f) Let's go outside for some fresh air.

   g) I hung the picture there yesterday.

   h) It was a warm day, so we ate lunch outdoors.

2. Find and circle more than one adverb that describes **where** in each sentence below.

   a) When it rains outside, we play indoors at recess.

   b) This bus goes east, and that bus travels west.


© Chalkboard Publishing

1. Read the following paragraph. Circle the adverbs that describe **where**. Underline the adverbs that describe **how**. Put a box around the adverbs that describe **when**.

I walked quickly toward my school. I slept in late today and did not want to miss my math test. When I finally arrived at school, my teacher looked seriously at me and asked, "Why are you late Jonathan?" I looked inside the classroom. My classmates were all there, quietly writing their tests. I nervously answered my teacher and explained that I had accidentally slept in. She asked me to get a late slip first, and to hurry back after so I could write my test.

2. Write two sentences that include each type of adverb.

   a) Adverbs that describe where:

   _______________________________________________

   _______________________________________________

   b) Adverbs that describe how:

   _______________________________________________

   _______________________________________________

   c) Adverbs that describe when:

   _______________________________________________

   _______________________________________________

# Some Adverbs Describe How Often

An **adverb** describes a **verb**. Some adverbs describe **how often** an action happens.

*Example: Helen (always) wears her seat belt in the car.*
The adverb **always** describes **how often** Helen wears her seat belt.

Learn these adverbs that describe **how often** an action happens:

**constantly** (all the time)          **occasionally** (once in a while)
**frequently** (very often)            **seldom** (not very often)
**usually** (most of the time)         **rarely** (almost never)

1. In each sentence, circle the adverb that tells **how often** an action happens. Underline the **verb that the adverb describes**. Draw an arrow from the adverb to the **verb it describes**.

   a) Paula often visits her aunt and uncle.

   b) Sometimes I play tag with my brother and sister.

   c) I never forget my grandmother's birthday.

   d) Jason sneezed twice today.

2. In each second sentence, use one of the **adverbs** from the list above. Choose an adverb that **does not** change the meaning of the first sentence.

   a) The tap drips all the time.          The tap drips ___________________________.

   b) He jogs not very often.          He ___________________________ jogs.

   c) She almost never yells.          She ___________________________ yells.

   d) Once in a while I cough.          ___________________________ I cough.

   e) We blink very often.          We blink ___________________________.

   f) Most of the time, I do my homework as soon as I get home.

      I ___________________________ do my homework as soon as I get home.

# Adverbs Review Quiz

1. Circle the adverbs that describe **how** an action happens. Some sentences have **more than one**.

   a) The frightened cat quickly darted across the lawn.

   b) The lightning bolt lit up the night sky brightly.

   c) Ted boldly approached the boy who took his hat and politely asked for it back.

   d) The stray dog timidly and slowly crept toward the stranger's outstretched hand.

2. Underline the adverbs that describe **when** an action happens. Some sentences have **more than one**.

   a) Ahmed is going to the mall after he leaves work on this evening.

   b) Julie came to my house yesterday to study for the test we have today.

   c) My aunt and uncle went dancing for their anniversary last summer.

   d) Ari's sister starts her driving lessons this weekend.

3. Put a box around the adverbs that describe **where** an action happens. Some sentences have **more than one**.

   a) The ants were inside the picnic basket and all over the food.

   b) Spiders can be found worldwide, even in the Arctic and Antarctic.

   c) I looked throughout the house for my keys, but I couldn't find them anywhere.

   d) The dog ran upstairs during the thunderstorm and hid underneath the bed.

   e) The scientists dug below the bridge and found ancient tools inside an old clay jar.

4. Circle the adverbs that describe **how often** an action happens. Some sentences have **more than one**.

   a) I sometimes forget to bring my sweater to baseball practice.

   b) My grandmother always sends me a card on my birthday.

   c) Jill and I jumped the skipping rope fifty-five times without stopping.

   d) I have never walked past the graveyard. Not even once.

5. Replace the words in brackets with an adverb that **means the same**.

   a) Mrs. Kahn __________ drops by to have tea and cookies with my mother. (very often)

   b) Our postal worker __________ brings a package for me. (once in a while)

   c) Dad shops near his work, so he __________ goes to this new store. (almost never)

   d) We __________ walk by the firehall on our way to school. (most of the time)

6. Circle whether the adverb describes **when**, **where**, **how**, or **how often**.

   a) I practice my violin daily so I can play my best.  *when   where   how   how often*

   b) I pat my cat gently so she will purr for me.  *when   where   how   how often*

   c) Tammy takes ballet in that building.  *when   where   how   how often*

   d) When Michel juggles, he never drops a ball.  *when   where   how   how often*

   e) Sarah happily tried on her sister's dress.  *when   where   how   how often*

   f) Lars puts out the garbage on Friday mornings.  *when   where   how   how often*

   g) My cousin Katie and I ride horses in the forest.  *when   where   how   how often*

   h) On weekends, Sanjay jogs for exercise.  *when   where   how   how often*

# Exploring Types of Sentences

A **statement** is a sentence that ends with a **period**.

*Example: Ken goes to the park.*

A **question** is a sentence that ends with a **question mark**.

*Example: Would you like to go to the park?*

An **exclamation** is a sentence that shows strong feeling such as excitement, joy, or anger ends with an **exclamation mark**.

*Examples: I love the park!     Ouch!     I can't wait!*

A **command** is a sentence that tells someone to do something. It can end with a **period** or with an **exclamation mark**.

*Examples: Take off your boots.     Watch out!*

---

1. Write the **correct punctuation** at the end of each sentence.

   a) Would you like some apple slices____

   b) Put the salad bowl on the table____

   c) Hooray, we are going to the movies____

   d) Are you going to the museum today____

   e) The girls are working on a project____

   f) Be careful____

   g) When is your birthday____

   h) Help me clear the table, please____

2. Write three examples of **each type of sentence**. Be sure to include the **correct punctuation** at the end of each sentence.

a) A statement:

b) A question:

c) An exclamation:

d) A command:

3. Identify the type of sentence. Add the correct **punctuation mark** at the end of each sentence. Write the sentence type.

a) I had a fantastic day____

   Sentence type: _______________________________

b) What is your favorite color____

   Sentence type: _______________________________

c) Our new neighbors moved in yesterday____

   Sentence type: _______________________________

d) I love my new kitten so much____

   Sentence type: _______________________________

e) Brush your teeth before going to bed____

   Sentence type: _______________________________

f) My teacher's name is Mrs. Simpson____

   Sentence type: _______________________________

g) How did the rabbit get out of its cage____

   Sentence type: _______________________________

h) Take out the garbage____

   Sentence type: _______________________________

i) The baby is sleeping in her crib____

   Sentence type: _______________________________

# Complete Subjects

There are two parts to a sentence. These parts are called the **complete subject** and the **complete predicate**. We will talk about complete predicates in another lesson.

## Complete Subject

The **complete subject** contains all the words that tell **who or what** the sentence is about. In the examples below, the complete subject is in bold.

*Example:* ***A small gray cloud*** *drifted slowly across the sky.*

This sentence is about a cloud. The complete subject contains **all** the words that tell about the cloud.

*Example:* ***Our big maple tree*** *provides cool shade all summer long.*

This sentence is about a tree. The complete subject contains **all** the words that tell about the tree.

1. In each sentence, underline all the words in the **complete subject**.

   a) The red car drove toward the parking lot.

   b) Millions of stars twinkled in the night sky.

   c) The girl with the broken leg used crutches to walk.

   d) Our friends from Halifax arrived yesterday.

   e) The bread my mother made tastes delicious.

   f) Sasha's speech about the solar system went perfectly today.

   g) The long-haired dog was washed in the bathtub.

   h) The busy squirrels gathered lots of acorns for the winter.

   i) The strap on Terry's backpack broke on the school bus.

2. In each sentence, draw a **vertical line** after the **complete subject**.

   *Example: My favorite author | writes suspenseful mystery stories.*

   a) The flower garden at the school was planted by our class.

   b) Spaghetti and meatballs are a favorite dinner at Mario's house.

   c) The smell of hot apple pie drifted through the window.

   d) Red flowers in my mother's garden attract lots of tiny hummingbirds.

   e) The soil in our composter is full of wiggling earthworms.

   f) Large furry fruit bats are called flying foxes.

   g) Some types of whales swim north in summer.

3. Identify whether the **bold part** of the sentence is a **complete subject**. Circle **Yes** or **No**.

   a) **The silly clowns at the circus** tripped and fell all over each other.   **Yes   No**

   b) My cat likes to **lie in the sun for hours and sleep**.   **Yes   No**

   c) The library book I am reading **is an exciting adventure story**.   **Yes   No**

   d) **Han and his family** went fishing on the lake last weekend.   **Yes   No**

   e) **Our dinner on a hot day** includes potato salad, tomato wedges, and fresh pita bread.
   **Yes   No**

   f) A big group of happy children **had fun at the playground**.   **Yes   No**

   g) **The long tail of the lemur** helps the animal balance as it leaps across the ground.
   **Yes   No**

   h) **Desserts that turn out messy or wrong** still taste good.   **Yes   No**

# Complete Predicates

In a previous lesson, we talked about complete subject of a sentence, which tells who or what the sentence is about. Now we will talk about the rest of the sentence: The **complete predicate**.

The **complete predicate** includes the **verb** and **all** the words that tell about what happened in the sentence. In the examples below, the complete predicate is underlined.

*Example: The tall tree swayed dangerously in the strong wind.*

The verb in this sentence is *swayed*. The other underlined words help to tell about what happened in the sentence.

*Example: The box of beads spilled all over the floor.*

The verb in this sentence is *spilled*. The other underlined words help to tell about what happened in the sentence.

Every word in a sentence will be part the complete subject **or** part of the complete predicate. In the examples below, the complete subject is in bold, and the complete predicate is underlined.

*Examples: **Happy children** blew bubbles in the park.*
*          **The robins in our backyard** are building a nest again this year.*

---

1. In each sentence, underline all the words in the **complete predicate**.

    a) The birthday cake tasted delicious.

    b) Bill and Vivian watched the fireworks last night.

    c) A school of fish swam together in the ocean.

    d) The children watch cartoons on Saturday mornings.

    e) My new shoes make running much easier.

    f) The tall silver ladder leans against the brick wall.

    g) Wild raspberries in the woods ripen in the middle of summer.

    h) Tufts of fur grow between the toes of my friend's fluffy cat.

2. In each sentence, draw a **vertical line** before the **complete predicate**.

   *Example: My favorite music* | *makes me want to dance.*

   a) Furry bats can be found in all shapes and sizes.

   b) Most North American bats eat only insects.

   c) Some bats from Mexico drink the nectar from certain types of cactus flowers.

   d) These nectar bats cross the border into the United States at night.

   e) Cactus flowers in the Arizona desert near Mexico provide food for nectar bats.

   f) These bats eat sugar water from hummingbird feeders, too.

   g) People in Arizona find their hummingbird feeders are empty in the morning.

3. Identify whether the **bold part** of the sentence is a **complete predicate**.
   Circle **Yes** or **No**.

   a) On hot summer days, **drink plenty of water**.  *Yes*  *No*

   b) **Bees and other flying bugs** swarm around the flowering trees in our yard.  *Yes*  *No*

   c) The silly cat **climbed the neighbor's tree and got stuck**.  *Yes*  *No*

   d) **People must walk** carefully so they do not slip on icy sidewalks in winter.  *Yes*  *No*

   e) **Butterflies and moths** flutter their wings when they fly.  *Yes*  *No*

   f) The skunk in our neighborhood **sprayed the neighbor's dog last night**.  *Yes*  *No*

   g) My dog Hugo **chewed his toy so it will no longer roll**.  *Yes*  *No*

   h) **Sweet and sticky honey** dripped all over the table.  *Yes*  *No*

# Avoiding Sentence Fragments

A **sentence** contains a **complete idea.** To write a complete idea, you need two things:

**1.** Someone or something that is doing an action
**2.** The action that someone or something is doing

If one or both of these things are missing, you have a **sentence fragment.**
Add the missing part to create a sentence with a complete idea.

*Examples:*

a) *The boy with long black hair.*
   This is a **sentence fragment**. It does not tell what **action** the boy is doing.

   *The boy with long black hair sharpened his pencil.*
   This is a **sentence**. It tells what **action** the boy is doing.

b) *Walked up the stairs as quiet as a mouse.*
   This is a **sentence fragment**. It does not tell **who** is walking up the stairs.

   *The burglar walked up the stairs as quiet as a mouse.*
   This is a **sentence**. It tells **who** is doing the action.

c) *Way up high at the top of a tree.*
   This is a **sentence fragment**. It does not tell who or what is **doing an action**, and it does not tell **what the action is**.

   *A bird sang way up high at the top of a tree.*
   This is a **sentence**. It tells **what is doing the action** and **what the action is**.

Remember to check your writing to make sure each sentence contains a **complete idea**. Revise any sentence fragments you find to create a sentence with a complete idea.

    

1. What is missing in each **sentence fragment** below? Circle the answer.

   a) The new girl in our class.

   ***who or what is doing the action***     ***the action***     ***both are missing***

   b) Ran down the hall and out the door.

   ***who or what is doing the action***     ***the action***     ***both are missing***

   c) Inside Ken's bedroom closet.

   ***who or what is doing the action***     ***the action***     ***both are missing***

   d) The dog with the sad eyes.

   ***who or what is doing the action***     ***the action***     ***both are missing***

   e) Painted the window frame.

   ***who or what is doing the action***     ***the action***     ***both are missing***

   f) On the kitchen counter.

   ***who or what is doing the action***     ***the action***     ***both are missing***

2. Write **S** if it is a **sentence** (a complete idea) or **SF** if it is a **sentence fragment**.

   a) Long ago in a faraway land. _______

   b) The woman smiled. _______

   c) The police car with the flashing lights. _______

   d) Moving slowly through the dark forest. _______

   e) The kitten mewed softly. _______

   f) Over in the field behind the barn. _______

3. Rewrite **sentence fragments** from Question 2. Add what is missing to make each one a complete sentence. (Use your own ideas.)

a) _______________________________________________

_______________________________________________

b) _______________________________________________

_______________________________________________

c) _______________________________________________

_______________________________________________

d) _______________________________________________

_______________________________________________

e) _______________________________________________

_______________________________________________

4. Read the first word with each part, one at a time. **Two parts** make the sentence fragment into a **complete sentence**. Cross out the part that **does not**.

*Example:*

| *June...* | *is my favorite month.* | ~~*and July.*~~ | *is the start of summer.* |

| a) Billy... | and his dog. | jogs on the beach. | rides his bike to school. |
| b) Sari... | waved at me. | and I. | finished her homework. |
| c) Something... | on the shelf. | scratched my arm. | ate my sandwich. |
| d) My... | room is warm. | notebook and pen. | hair has been brushed. |

# Avoiding Run-On Sentences

A **run-on** sentence contains two complete ideas that are **not** correctly joined together. Look at the example below.

*Example: I studied hard I passed the test.*

Notice that "I studied hard" is a complete idea, and "I passed the test." is a complete idea. How could you correct this sentence?

You could use **a comma and a joining word** to join the ideas.

*Example: I studied hard**, and** I passed the test.*

You could **add a period** to make two separate sentences.

*Example: I studied hard. I passed the test.*

Remember that you **cannot** join two complete ideas with just a comma.

*Example: I thought I got cut, it was just a bruise.*

To correct the sentence, you could **add a joining word** after the comma.

*Example: I though I got cut, **but** it was just a bruise.*

You could **add a period** to make two separate sentences.

*Example: I thought I got cut. It was just a bruise.*

You **should not** join two complete ideas by using a joining word and no comma.

*Example: It was raining so I took my umbrella.*

When you use a joining word to join two complete ideas, make sure you use a **comma before** the joining word.

*Example: It was raining, **so** I took my umbrella.*

Always check your writing for run-on sentences. Correct any run-on sentences you find.

Remember that you can use a period to make two complete ideas into two separate sentences.

You can also use a comma **and** a joining word such as **and**, **but**, **or**, or **so** to connect two complete ideas in a sentence.

1. For each sentence below, write **RO** if it is a run-on sentence. Put a **check mark** if the sentence is correct.

   a) Jackson threw the ball it went over the fence. _______

   b) I don't need a jacket it is warm outside. _______

   c) The house was on fire and the fire trucks came quickly. _______

   d) The lamp wasn't working, so I replaced the lightbulb. _______

   e) Shara was going to play basketball with us but she hurt her foot. _______

   f) Istvan could take the dog for a walk or Kara might want to do it. _______

2. Show **two** ways to correct each **run-on sentence**. Look at the example.

   *Example: Dad did not mow the grass this week, it grew long.*
   *Dad did not mow the grass this week. It grew long.*
   *Dad did not mow the grass this week, so it grew long.*

   a) I forgot my pencil I have another one.

   __________________________

   __________________________

   b) The dog is outside it needs to come in.

   __________________________

   __________________________

   c) My sister washed the dishes I dried them.

   __________________________

   __________________________

# Conjunctions: *And, But, Or,* and *So*

A **conjunction** is used to join together two ideas or sentences.

We use the conjunction **and** to join together two ideas that are related.
*Example: I like apples, and I like pears.*

We use the conjunction **but** to join together two ideas that go against each other.
*Example: I like apples, but I do not like apple juice.*

We use the conjunction **or** to join together two ideas where only one idea can happen.
*Example: We can have apple juice, or we can have orange juice.*

We use the conjunction **so** to join together two ideas that happen because of each other.
*Example: We had some apple juice, so I drank it.*

1. Use **and** or **but** to fill in the blank.

   a) I like to go for bike rides, _________ I like to go swimming.

   b) I like to watch funny movies, _______ I do not like to watch scary movies.

   c) My sister is older than I am, _______ I am smarter.

   d) I like to read mystery novels, _______ I like to read fantasy novels.

2. Use **or** or **so** to fill in the blank.

   a) We can have spaghetti for dinner, ______ we can have pizza.

   b) The restaurant did not have spaghetti, ______ we got pizza.

   c) The store did not have a red backpack, _______ I got a blue one.

   d) We can go to the movie theater, ______ we can go to the amusement park.

# Conjunctions: *Since, Because, Until, Before, After, While, When,* and *As Soon As*

Use **conjunctions** to join together two ideas. Below is a list of more conjunctions that can help join together different ideas.

***Since*** or ***because****: Used to join together an idea that **explains another idea**.
*Examples: I am very happy because it is the day before my birthday.*
       *Tim has been very sad since his dog ran away.*

***Until****: Used to join together an idea that was happening with **an idea that interrupted it**.
*Example: I was riding my bike until my friend asked me to go swimming.*

***Before*** or ***after****: Used to join together two ideas that happened **before** or **after** each other.
*Example: I was riding my bike before my friends came over.*

***While****: Used to join together two ideas that are happening at the **same time**.
*Example: Dad was brushing his teeth while he showered.*

***When****: Used to join together an idea that was happening with **an idea that interrupted it.**
*Example: I was playing outside when it started to rain.*

***As soon as****: Used to join together ideas that happen **one after the other**.
*Example: I will go to the store as soon as my mom gives me money for milk.*

---

Fill in the blank with the correct **conjunction**.

a) I was walking to the store _____________ it started to rain. (since   when)

b) I was reading a book _____________ I took my dog for a walk. (until   because)

c) I got dressed ___________ I got out of bed. (while   after)

d) My sister used the computer _____________ she got home. (as soon as   while)

e) I watched TV _____________ I did my homework. (because   while)

f) My friend needs to go home soon _________ it is getting dark. (after   because)

# Prepositions

A **preposition** is a type of word that helps join parts of a sentence.

Use a preposition **before a noun** or **pronoun**.
Most prepositions tell about **time**, **place**, or **movement**

Examples: Time: **after, before, by, during, from, on, past, since, through, to, until**
Place: **above, behind, below, beside, between, by, inside, near, on, over**
Movement: **against, along, down, from, into, around, out of, toward, up**

---

Fill in the blank with the correct **preposition**.

a) After school on Friday, my friends and I are going _____________ the mall.

b) Over the winter holidays, some of my family will come to visit _____________ Boston.

c) My teacher asked me to get some crayons. They are _____________ the cupboard.

d) I like to eat vegetables _____________ ranch dip.

e) My favorite books are about Harry Potter. They are written _________ J.K. Rowling.

f) I left my homework _____________ home today by accident.

g) My grandma left her dentures _____________ the night table while she took a nap.

h) I got my mother a nice present _____________ Mother's Day.

i) I always wash my hands _____________ I eat dinner.

j) Earth orbits _____________ the Sun.

# Sentences Review Quiz

1. Write the **sentence type** beside each sentence (statement, command, question, or exclamation). Add the **correct punctuation mark** at the end of the sentence.

   a) Put your dirty clothes in the hamper___      _______________________________________

   b) Will Pete be coming with us___      _________________________________

   c) I wonder if it will rain today___      ______________________________

   d) Mud splashed all over me___      _______________________________

2. In each sentence, draw a **vertical line** between the **complete subject** and the **complete predicate**.

   a) There are fifteen wild geese eating grass in the park across the road.

   b) The tiny brown mouse chewed through the cereal box.

   c) An interesting program on elephants shows on television tonight.

   d) This kitchen drawer sticks shut every time.

3. Beside each sentence below, write **S** if it is a **sentence** or **SF** if it is a **sentence fragment**.

   a) My cousin's bicycle.  ________

   b) I like freckles.  ________

   c) Her long brown hair.  ________

   d) Half the kids sing well.  ________

4. Write **RO** if it is a **run-on sentence**. Put a **check mark** if the sentence is correct.

   a) Zara has the measles so she has to stay home from school. ________

   b) Her perfume smells spicy I do not like the smell. ________

     © Chalkboard Publishing

c) The thunder is loud and the dog is afraid. ________

d) We have volleyball practice today, but I feel sick. ________

5. Write the **correct conjunction**. Use *and*, *but*, *or*, or *so*.

   a) My little brother was sick last night, _______ he is sleeping late this morning.

   b) We are twins, _______ I am two minutes older than my sister.

   c) Cathy and Maya baked cookies, _______ they also baked muffins.

   d) We can play basketball, _______ we can play frisbee.

6. Write the **correct conjunction** from the words in brackets.

   a) I set the table ___________ my mother put the supper on plates. (because  while)

   b) I was reading an intense part in my book, __________ the phone rang and scared me. (before  when)

   c) My brother and I ran to answer the door ____________ my cousins arrived. (as soon as   until)

   d) Tom felt a bit sick ____________ eating too much ice cream. (before  after)

7. Choose the **correct preposition** from the words in brackets.

   a) ________ the test on Friday, I was very happy that it was over. (During  After)

   b) Maxine went to the dentist and found out she had a cavity ___________ two teeth. (near   between)

   c) My cousins are here visiting us ___________ London, England. (through  from)

   d) The mouse was afraid, so it ran __________ the wall to avoid the cat. (between   along)

# Punctuating Dialogue

Use **quotation marks** around words that someone is speaking.

*Examples: "Please hand in your papers," <u>the teacher said</u>.*
*"I have a secret," <u>whispered Sally</u>.*
*"Come play soccer with us!" <u>shouted Manuel</u>.*

The underlined words are called **speaker tags**. A speaker tag tells who is talking. When the speaker tag comes **after** the spoken words, remember to put a comma **before** the **second** quotation mark.

When the speaker tag comes **after** the spoken words, **do not** put a **comma** before the second quotation mark if there is a **question mark** or **exclamation point** at the end of the spoken words.

*Examples: "Who left the door open**?**" asked Ray.*
*"That is so amazing**!**" exclaimed Shauna.*

If the speaker tag comes **before** the spoken words, put a comma **after** the speaker tag.
*Example: The baker said**,** "This bread is very fresh."*
Remember to use a **capital letter** for the first spoken word.

---

1. Add **quotation marks** to each sentence below. Add a **comma**, if necessary.

a) We won the game!    shouted Mary.

b) I hope we have good weather during our vacation    Dad said.

c) I wonder if she noticed that we came in late    whispered Beth.

d) Would you like to look through the telescope?    the scientist asked.

e) The police officer said    We have caught the thief.

f)  Does he know we are following him?    asked the spy.

g) The children said    We always have fun at the beach.

h) Aaron nervously said    The wind has really picked up!

i) Leann exclaimed    That new haircut looks great on you!

2. Add **quotation marks** to each sentence. Add a **comma** or **other punctuation** where necessary.

a) That bird flew right over my head     shouted Yu.

b) Danny asked   Does anyone know where the scrap paper is kept?

c) Miss Henry said   Open your books and turn to page 19.

d) Sand is stuck all over me     complained Minnie.

e) Mom warned   Make sure you look both ways before you cross the street.

f) I have an idea for a Father's Day gift for Dad   Kevin whispered.

g) How is Benny feeling today     Mrs. Martinez asked Mom.

3. Add **quotation marks** and **all** the correct **punctuation** to each sentence. Read the sentence carefully and watch for abbreviations.

a) Have you seen the new skateboard Ashley got   asked Todd

b) Move away from the door   Mom said to our dog

c) Karen groaned   I have so much homework to do

d) I won the spelling bee   Tim announced

e) Cathy asked     Why is this door open

f) That cloud looks like a teddy bear     said May

g) Can anyone tell us the answer     asked Mrs  Turnbull

h) Amy whispered     Do you see the baby birds in the nest on that branch

i) Mr  Green said   Please help me carry these packages to the car

4. Maxine and Aaron are planning a surprise for their mother's birthday. Write the dialogue for their secret discussion.

________________________________________________________________________

________________________________________________________________________

________________________________________________________________________

________________________________________________________________________

________________________________________________________________________

________________________________________________________________________

5. John and Arvin are walking to the park to join a baseball team. Write the excited dialogue that occurs on their way there.

________________________________________________________________________

________________________________________________________________________

________________________________________________________________________

________________________________________________________________________

________________________________________________________________________

________________________________________________________________________

# Abbreviations

An **abbreviation** is the **short form** of a word. An abbreviation ends with a **period**. The abbreviations in the sentence below are in bold.

*Mrs.* *Chapman drove* *Mr.* *Pappas to the store.*

**Mrs.** is the abbreviation of *mistress*, and **Mr.** is the abbreviation of *mister*.

Below are two abbreviations you probably have seen before.

*Dr.* *Ellis lives at 32 Talbot* *St.*

**Dr.** is the abbreviation of *doctor*, and **St.** is the abbreviation of *street*.

Use **Dr.** only before someone's name. Look at the examples below.

*Example: I am going to see* *Dr.* *Glinski tomorrow.*

**Dr.** comes before the last name *Glinski*, so it is correct to use the abbreviation of **doctor**.

*Example: A* *doctor* *lives next door to us.*

In this sentence, **doctor** does **not** come before someone's name, so it would **not** be correct to use the abbreviation **Dr**.

Use **St.** only when it comes after the **name** of a street.

*Example: Carolyn lives at 234 Simcoe* *St.*

**St.** comes after the name of a street, so it is correct to use the abbreviation.

*Example: I live on a* *street* *that is close to the park.*

**Street** does **not** come after the name of a street, so it would **not** be correct to use the abbreviation in this sentence.

Below are two more abbreviations you see in addresses. Like **St.**, use these abbreviations **only** when they come after a name.

| Word | Abbreviation | Example |
|------|--------------|---------|
| avenue | Ave. | *We are moving to 27 Brentwood* **Ave.** |
| road | Rd. | *The school is on Oak* **Rd.** |

1. Circle the **correct choice** in brackets.

   a) I have an appointment to see ( doctor  Dr. ) Jones tomorrow.

   b) We drove up a long and winding ( road  Rd. ) to get there.

   c) Turn right when you get to Elm ( street  St.) and you'll see the library.

   d) They saw a long ( avenue  Ave. ) with street lamps on both sides.

   e) Is ( doctor  Dr. )  Ricci the only ( doctor  Dr. ) in the office right now?

   f) On Fanshaw Park ( road  Rd. ), there is a lot of construction.

   g) Did you forget which ( street  St. ) your piano teacher lives on?

   h) The apartment complex on Chartwell ( avenue  Ave. ) has a large playground.

2. Check for the correct use of abbreviations. If there are errors, write the **correct sentence** on the line. If there are no errors, put a check mark beside the sentence.

   a) Doctor Lindzon spoke at a seminar with mrs Lopez.

   _______________________________________________________

   b) York Ave. is near Orchard Park Public School.

   _______________________________________________________

   c) How close is Waterside Rd to the office where mr. Castle works?

   _______________________________________________________

   d) Are there lots of trees on your st.?

   _______________________________________________________

# Using Commas in Lists

A sentence can contain a **list**. If the list has **more than two** items, use a **comma** after each item **except** the last item.

*Example: We put <u>strawberries</u>, <u>bananas</u>, and <u>oranges</u> in the bowl.*

Each item in a list can be **more than one word**. Use a **comma** after each item **except** the last item.

*Example: We walked <u>down the hill</u>, <u>across the orchard</u>, and <u>down the road</u> on our way home.*

1. Add **commas** to the list in each sentence.

   a) Brady's favorite snacks are bananas crackers and cheese.

   b) My favorite shirt has blue green and yellow stripes.

   c) Andrew Evan and Ella are in the Environment Club.

   d) Wednesday Thursday and Friday are track and field practice days.

   e) Emma asked Emile Sheena and Leo to come over after school.

   f) My parents like to play in tennis volleyball and soccer leagues.

2. Add **commas** to these lists that are **more than one word**.

   a) Hanna washed the car cut the grass and took out the garbage.

   b) The bird flew over the fence across the yard and into the maple tree

   c) My sister my brother and I helped to shovel the snow.

   d) I spend most of my time attending school doing homework and playing with my friends.

   e) Eat breakfast get enough sleep and exercise to stay healthy.

   f) I want to finish my homework play outside and call my friend before bedtime.

# Contractions with *Have* and *Had*

A **contraction** is one word made from two words, with one or more of the letters **left out**. The letters that are left out are replaced with an **apostrophe**.

Look below to see contractions made with the words *have* and *had*.

## Contractions with *Have*

| Two Words | Contraction |
| --- | --- |
| I have | I've |
| you have | you've |

| Two Words | Contraction |
| --- | --- |
| we have | we've |
| they have | they've |

## Contractions with *Had*

| Two Words | Contraction |
| --- | --- |
| I had | I'd |
| you had | you'd |
| he had | he'd |

| Two Words | Contraction |
| --- | --- |
| she had | she'd |
| we had | we'd |
| they had | they'd |

Complete each sentence by writing the **contraction** for the words in brackets.

a) ______________ forgotten his name. (I have)

b) ______________ eaten two bananas already. (She had)

c) I heard that ______________ gone on vacation. (they have)

d) We would have helped you if ______________ been there. (we had)

e) I wish ______________ studied harder for the test. (I had)

f) That is the third book ______________ read this week. (you have)

g) We did not realize ______________ already gone. (they had)

# Contractions with *Not*

Look below to see **contractions** made with the word *not*.

| Two Words | Contraction |
| --- | --- |
| are not | aren't |
| cannot | can't |
| could not | couldn't |
| did not | didn't |
| do not | don't |
| does not | doesn't |
| had not | hadn't |
| has not | hasn't |

| Two Words | Contraction |
| --- | --- |
| have not | haven't |
| is not | isn't |
| must not | mustn't |
| should not | shouldn't |
| was not | wasn't |
| were not | weren't |
| will not | won't |
| would not | wouldn't |

In each sentence, write the **contraction** for the words in brackets.

a) You _________________ forget to water the plants. (must not)

b) I _________________ wear sandals on a cold day. (would not)

c) Leon _________________ forgotten to brush his teeth. (had not)

d) We _________________ be going to see the play. (will not)

e) Margaret _________________ go swimming by herself. (should not)

f) The children _________________ walk any farther. (could not)

g) They _________________ seen Paul since yesterday. (have not)

h) Mr. Chen _________________ find his cat. (cannot)

i) We _________________ enjoying this scary movie. (are not)

# Using *There*, *Their*, and *They're*

*There*, *their*, and *they're* all sound alike. Make sure you write the correct word! Look at the definitions below.

| Word | Definition and Example |
|------|------------------------|
| there | a place<br>*Example: I would like to travel **there** one day.* |
| their | a possessive pronoun that means **belonging to them**<br>*Example: They hung up **their** coats in the closet.* |
| they're | the contraction of the words **they are**<br>*Example: **They're** excited about playing the new video game.* |

Complete each sentence with the correct word or words (***there***, ***their***, or ***they're***).

a) _______________ aunt and uncle live in Hawaii.

b) _______________ going to go shopping after lunch.

c) Trish saw a snake right _______________ by the tree.

d) The birds flew away because _______________ afraid of the cat.

e) I sometimes go _______________ when take the dog for a walk.

f) The rabbits are cute, and I like to pet _______________ soft fur.

g) We'll plant tulips here, and we'll plant daisies over _______________.

h) Birds sit on _______________ eggs to keep them warm.

i) _______________ going to ask _______________ friends to come, too.

j) Let's go to _______________ house to see if _______________ home.

k) _______________ going to have fun when they get _______________.

# Using Capital Letters in Titles

Use **capital letters** when you write the title of a book, story, poem, song, or movie.

**Rule 1:** Use a capital letter for the first letter of all **nouns, pronouns, adjectives, verbs,** and **adverbs**. Most words in a title will be one of these.

*Examples: Three Blind Mice    Charlotte's Web*

**Rule 2: Do not** use a capital letter for the first letter in these short words, **unless** they are the **first or last word** in the title:

**a   an   and   by   for   in   of   on   the   to   up   with**

*Examples: Harry Potter and the Goblet of Fire    The Farmer in the Dell*

**Rule 3: Always** use a capital letter for the **first and last words** in a title, no matter what the word is.

*Examples: Let the Sunshine In    Polly Put the Kettle On*

---

1. Use **capital letters** where necessary to write the titles below.

   a) james and the giant peach _______________________________________

   b) dancing in the street _______________________________________

   c) the indian in the cupboard _______________________________________

   d) the wizard of oz _______________________________________

   e) a chair for my mother _______________________________________

   f) down by the lake _______________________________________

2. Write the titles of **one book** and **one movie** you like. Do not choose a title that already appears on this page. Use capital letters where necessary.

   a) book: _______________________________________

   b) movie: _______________________________________

# Write the Correct Word

Don't be confused by the words below. Check your writing to make sure you have chosen the correct words.

| Word | Definition and Example |
|------|------------------------|
| its | a possessive pronoun that means **belonging to it** <br> *Example: The tree has lost all **its** leaves.* |
| it's | the contraction of the words **it is** <br> *Example: **It's** going to be a sunny day.* |
| then | next or afterward <br> *Example: I'll make a sandwich, and **then** I'll eat it.* |
| than | a word used when comparing two or more things <br> *Example: The red socks are warmer **than** the blue socks.* |
| maybe | perhaps or possibly <br> *Example: **Maybe** the rain will stop soon.* |
| may be | might be <br> *Example: They **may be** home, but I'm not sure.* |

In each sentence, circle the **correct choice** in the brackets.

a) I like pears better ( than  then ) plums.

b) The playful puppy had fun chasing ( its  it's ) tail.

c) I think Parker ( maybe  may be ) at hockey practice now.

d) The train slowed down, and ( than  then ) it finally stopped.

e) The weather report said ( its  it's ) going to snow today.

f) Our new computer has a bigger screen ( than  then ) the old one.

g) ( Its  It's ) sad that the baby bird fell from ( its  it's ) nest.

h) ( Maybe  May be ) you are wrong, but you ( maybe  may be ) right.

# Correcting Errors: *Boa Constrictors*

Find and correct **16 errors** in this text.

1   A boa constrictor is a type of snake. One of the longest snakes in the world. Some boas grow to be more than 13 feet (4 meters) long. Boa's live in the wild in warm countries such as mexico. Some people keep boas as pets. They feel that looking after a boa is easier then looking after other types of pets.

2   Most boas have skin that are different shades of brown. The colors on their skin help boas hide among dead leafs on the ground. Boas have different patterns on they're skin. One scientist said "There beautiful animals. I think boas have the most interesting patterns of all snakes.

3   A boa kills its prey by wrapping itself around an animals' body. Then it squeezes the animal. Squeezes so tight the animal cant breathe.

4   If a boa hisses, that means it maybe angry. Youd better be careful if a boa hisses at you. Boas are not poisonous but they can still bite!

Find and correct **14 errors** in this text.

1   One day, Dad and I was at the grocery store. Dad picked up a tin of dog food. "Do you think fred will like this?," he asked. I looked at the label.

> **BEEFY STEW**
>
> It's a meal your dog will love!

2   "Fred will eat anything," I said. "Im sure he'll love it." Dad put the tin in the shopping cart with the other grocerys.

3   The next day, Mom gave us stew for lunch. It looked strange, and it smelled even worse then it looked.

4   "This is the smellyest stew ever!", I said.

5   Dad tasted a spoonful. I could tell from his face that he did'nt like it.

6   "What kind of stew is this? he asked Mom.

7   Mom got the tin, and then she read the label. "Its called Beefy Stew" she said. Dad and me couldn't stop laughing.

8   Fred has a good dinner that night. The label was right. He loved Beefy Stew!

# Vocabulary List 1

## accurate

*(adjective)* correct in measure, detail, or information; exact; capable or successful in reaching the intended target
*Example: Robin Hood's archery skills were extremely **accurate**, and he always hit the bullseye.*

---

## eager

*(adjective)* wanting very much to do or to have something; keenly interested or expecting something
*Example: Tom raced to the front door because he was **eager** to see his grandparents.*

---

## flexible

*(adjective)* able to bend easily; ready and able to change to adapt to different situations
*Example: I have a job, so I can only go to the movies on Wednesdays. Mary isn't working, so her time is more **flexible**.*

---

## descend

*(verb)* to move or fall downward; to make a sudden attack on someone or something
Example: The cat **descended** on the tiny mouse hiding in the grass and caught it.

---

## impact

*(noun)* the action of one object coming into violent contact with another object
*Example: The **impact** of the meteorite crashing to Earth made a huge crater in the ground.*

---

## recent

*(adjective)* having happened, started, or been done not long ago
*Example: The puppy was a **recent** addition to their family, so they hadn't yet put a gate at the top of the stairs.*

---

## vacant

*(adjective)* having no fixtures, furniture, or inhabitants; empty
*Example: The parking lot was completely **vacant**, so we knew the movie theater was still closed.*

# Vocabulary List 1: Review

**accurate   eager   flexible   descent   impact   recent   vacant**

1. Write the **correct** vocabulary word beside each definition.

   a) ________________: having happened or been done not long ago

   b) ________________: having no fixtures, furniture, or inhabitants; empty

   c) ________________: correct in measure, detail, or information; exact

   d) ________________: the action of one object coming into violent contact with another

   e) ________________: to move or fall downward; to suddenly attack

   f) ________________: wanting very much to do or to have something

   g) ________________: ready and able to change to adapt; able to bend easily

2. Write the **correct** vocabulary word in each sentence. For **verbs**, remember to use
   the correct form (singular or plural) and the correct tense (past, present, or future).

   a) Rick measured the windows twice, so the size of the glass would be ___________.

   b) Cara's new haircut was a ______________ change to her looks.

   c) Gino was ______________ to show everyone the new dance he learned.

   d) Mrs. Baxter found a ______________ parking space close to the mall entrance.

   e) The ______________ of hitting the floor smashed the mirror into a million pieces.

   f) A swarm of locusts ________________ on the wheat field and ate all the plants.

   g) Alex had taken gymnastics since he was little, so he was very ______________.

 © Chalkboard Publishing

# Vocabulary List 2

**assist**

*(verb)* to help do something
*Example: My father and I **assisted** Mr. Brown when he moved to a new house.*

---

**blend**

*(verb)* to mix substances together into one smooth mixture
*Example: My mom and I **blended** some fruit and milk into smoothies this morning.*

*(noun)* something that is a mix of two or more substances
*Example: My new winter coat is made of a **blend** of cotton and wool.*

---

**frantic**

*(adjective)* wild with extreme upset, fear, worry, or panic; conducted in a hurried or mixed up way
*Example: Maria **frantically** banged on the door when she accidentally got locked outside in the snow.*

---

**lack**

*(verb)* to be without something, or not having enough of something
*Example: Theo's parties were dull because they always **lacked** good dance music.*

---

**peculiar**

*(adjective)* strange, odd, or unusual
*Example: When we walked into the crumbling house, we noticed a very **peculiar** smell.*

---

**reveal**

*(verb)* to make previously unknown or secret information known to other people
*Example: The last episode of the series **revealed** the identity of the art thief.*

**assist   blend   frantic   lack   peculiar   reveal**

1. Write the **correct** vocabulary word beside each definition. You may need to use some words more than once.

a) _________________________: wild with extreme upset, fear, worry, or panic

b) _________________________: to make secret information known to other people

c) _________________________: to be without something

d) _________________________: to mix substances together into one smooth mixture

e) _________________________: strange, odd, or unusual

f) _________________________: to help do something

g) _________________________: something that is a mix of two or more substances

2. Write the **correct** vocabulary word in each sentence. For **verbs**, remember to use the correct form (singular or plural) and the correct tense (past, present, or future).

a) The colors at first were separate, then they _______________ into a muddy brown.

b) The most _______________ thing happened when we visited my aunt this weekend.

c) The TV show we watched wasn't very good. It really _______________ suspense.

d) After the woman vanished, the magician _______________ where she went.

e) Our dog is a _______________ of poodle and Jack Russell terrier.

f) I need someone to _______________ me with carrying the trays of sandwiches.

g) The woman was _______________ when she dropped her keys into the sewer grate.

# Vocabulary List 3

**increase**

*(verb)* to become or make greater in size, amount, intensity, or degree
*Example: When you blow air into a balloon, the size of the balloon **increases**.*

*(noun)* an instance of growing or making greater in some way
*Example: My brother is a very hard worker, so he received an **increase** in pay.*

---

**sturdy**

*(adjective)* strong and solidly built
*Example: Cars can safely drive on the old wooden bridge because it is still very **sturdy**.*

---

**tidy**

*(adjective)* arranged neatly and in order
*Example: Mom said I can have a goldfish if keep my room neat and **tidy**.*

---

**frequent**

*(adjective)* happening often, many times, or very close together
*Example: The neighbor's cat comes to visit us **frequently** to get fed and patted.*

---

**outstanding**

*(adjective)* excellent; wonderful; superb
*Example: The ice skating team gave an **outstanding** performance and won the trophy.*

---

**release**

*(verb)* allow or enable to escape; set free
*Example: The hawk's wing had healed perfectly, so the rescuers **released** the bird back into the wild.*

# Vocabulary List 3: Review

**increase   sturdy   tidy   frequent   outstanding   release**

1. Write the **correct** vocabulary word beside each definition. You may need to use some words more than once.

a) _______________________: happening often or many times

b) _______________________: an instance of growing or making greater

c) _______________________: arranged neatly and in order

d) _______________________: allow or enable to escape; set free

e) _______________________: to become or make greater in size or intensity

f) _______________________: strong and solidly built

g) _______________________: excellent; wonderful; superb

2. Write the **correct** vocabulary word in each sentence. For **verbs**, remember to use the correct form (singular or plural) and the correct tense (past, present, or future).

a) My grandmother's house was always neat, clean, and _______________.

b) Tim's father helped us build a safe and _______________ treehouse in the yard.

c) If I continue to train, I will be able to _______________ the distance I can run.

d) When the weather is hot, we make _______________ trips to the beach.

e) My teacher said I did an _______________ job on my science project.

f) At special events, people sometimes _______________ white birds called doves.

g) Kim's little brother had a bigger _______________ in height than Kim did.

# Vocabulary List 4

**dusk**

(*noun*) the time when the daylight is nearly gone, just before it becomes night
*Example: The scouts started a campfire just before **dusk**, while they could still see.*

---

**portion**

(*noun*) an amount, section, or piece of something; part of a whole
*Example: My mother makes sure I have a child's **portion** of food at the restaurant.*

---

**prefer**

(*verb*) to like one thing better than another thing
*Example: I like all kinds of ice cream, but I really **prefer** chocolate ice cream.*

---

**recognize**

(*verb*) to identify someone or something from having seen it before
*Example: In my Grade 4 class, I **recognized** the girl who just moved onto my street.*

---

**severe**

(*adjective*) very bad or undesirable; intense; harsh; extreme
*Example: When Dale fell out of the tree, he went to the hospital because his injuries were **severe**.*

---

**queasy**

(*adjective*) feeling sick in the stomach
*Example: Going on the boat when the waves are high always makes my mother **queasy**.*

---

**resist**

(*verb*) to withstand the action or effect of something
*Example: Anyone who smelled Mom's fresh baked bread could not **resist** eating a piece.*

# Vocabulary List 4: Review

**dusk   portion   prefer   recognize   severe   queasy   resist**

1. Write the **correct** vocabulary word beside each definition.

a) ___________________________ : intense; harsh; extreme

b) ___________________________ : to withstand the action or effect of something

c) ___________________________ : feeling sick in the stomach

d) ___________________________ : to identify someone from having seen them before

e) ___________________________ : to like one thing better than another thing

f) ___________________________ : the time just before it becomes night

g) ___________________________ : an amount, section, or piece of something

2. Write the **correct** vocabulary word in each sentence. For **verbs**, remember to use the correct form (singular or plural) and the correct tense (past, present, or future).

a) My dad cut the watermelon up and gave each of us a small ________________.

b) When my brother came to visit us, our dog ________________ his voice immediately.

c) My mother likes rock and roll music, but my father ________________ jazz.

d) It is harder for drivers to see when driving at dawn and at ________________.

e) Just before I have to make a speech, I always feel ________________.

f) The weather report warned us of a ________________ thunderstorm this evening.

g) Aunt Julie couldn't ________________ adopting one of our cute kittens.

# Vocabulary List 5

**distract**

*(verb)* to prevent someone from giving full attention to something; to draw attention away from something
*Example: My brother tried to **distract** me by throwing things, so I wouldn't see him hide my pillow.*

---

**variety**

*(adjective)* a number of different types of things; things that are all different; lack of sameness
*Example: Our grocery store has a wide **variety** of delicious fruits and vegetables in summer.*

---

**source**

*(noun)* the person, place, or thing something comes from or can be obtained from
*Example: The **source** of the news story was a man who had been there when the accident happened.*

---

**sole**

*(noun)* the underside of a person's foot; the bottom of a shoe
*Example: The **soles** of her feet hurt from walking on the stony path.*

---

**indicate**

*(verb)* to point out; to show; to suggest a good or necessary path or course of action
*Example: The increase in clothing sales **indicates** that we should buy more of the new jeans.*

---

**jagged**

*(adjective)* having rough, sharp points sticking out
*Example: The mountain goat's feet make it easy for the animal to climb on **jagged**, rocky cliffs.*

# Vocabulary List 5: Review

**distract   variety   source   sole   indicate   jagged**

1. Write the **correct** vocabulary word beside each definition.

   a) _____________________________: having rough, sharp points sticking out

   b) _____________________________: to point out; to show

   c) _____________________________: a number of different types of things

   d) _____________________________: the bottom of a shoe

   e) _____________________________: to draw attention away from something

   f) _____________________________: the person, place, or thing something comes from

2. Write the **correct** vocabulary word in each sentence. For **verbs**, remember to use the correct form (singular or plural) and the correct tense (past, present, or future).

   a) The dark clouds and thunder _______________ that a storm is coming.

   b) The comic book store had a huge _______________ of superhero comics.

   c) Sandy cut her hand on a _______________ piece of broken glass.

   d) The _______________ of the water was an underground spring.

   e) Jill _______________ the dog with a squeaky toy, so Sam could catch the frightened animal.

   f) There were big holes in the _______________ of the old, worn-out boots.

# Grammar Review Test Grade 4

1. Circle all the **proper nouns**. Underline all the **common nouns**.

   a) Joey, Sari, and Ahmad went for a day at the zoo with their families.

   b) The Guggenheim Museum in New York has artworks by many famous artists.

   c) Pastor Henry works at the Anglican church by the river.

   d) On Tuesdays, we go shopping for groceries at Lucky Mart down the street.

2. Circle the **plural noun** in brackets that is **spelled correctly**. Some are tricky!

   a) We ate fresh juicy ( peachs   peaches ) for a snack today.

   b) Mia is reading a book about ( fairys   fairies ), ( trolls   trolles ), and ( elfs   elves ).

   c) In fall, we rake all the ( leafs   leaves ) into big ( piles   pilees ) and jump in them.

   d) The two ( chefs   cheves ) made a delicious dinner for the ( ladys   ladies ).

3. Write the correct **singular or plural possessive noun** for the words in brackets.

   a) Theo commented on how soft the ______________________________ felt.
   (paws of the kittens)

   b) The ______________________________ could be seen in the spilled flour.
   (footprints of the mouse)

   c) The old ______________________________ were yellowed with age. (pages of the book)

   d) The maple ______________________________ turned bright orange in the fall.
   (leaves of the trees)

4. Use the **correct pronoun** to replace the word or words in brackets.

   a) Sky and Roger wanted to go for a walk and I went with ____________.
   (Sky and Roger)

   b) We baked muffins for the fundraiser and ____________ smelled delicious.
   (the muffins)

c) Mom and Dad took _________________ out skiing on the weekend. (Sami and I)

d) Hanna wrote the quiz and _____________ got a great mark! (Hanna)

5. Cross out the **other person or people** in the sentence. Write the correct pronoun:
   *I* or *me*.

   a) Benny and _______ went to the store to buy bananas to make smoothies.

   b) Mrs. Smith bought boxes of cookies from Ana, Mike, and _______.

   c) My aunt's dogs came running toward _______ and Tom wagging their tails.

   d) Dusty, Cleo, and _______ played ball in my backyard.

6. Circle the correct form of the **verb** in brackets to make the **pronoun** and **verb**
   agree.

   a) Tia is coming over today. We always ( plays   play ) dominoes when she comes
      over.

   b) Terry is having fun with his friends. He ( plan   plans ) to go to the movies later.

   c) My big brother and sister are helpful. They ( help   helps ) me with my homework.

   d) My little cousin hopes to build a very tall block tower before it ( crash   crashes )
      down.

7. Write the correct **possessive pronoun** to replace the words in brackets.

   a) Our backyard is long and straight. _________________ is pie-shaped. (the backyard
      of the neighbors)

   b) My handwriting is neat, but _____________ is messy. (Janie's handwriting)

   c) My brother's tool chest if half full, but _____________ is full. (our uncle's tool chest)

   d) This notebook isn't _____________, it's _______________. (my notebook, the
      notebook belonging to you)

8. Use *a*, *an*, or *the*. Read the sentence to check if it talks about something **specific**.

   a) _______ large black spider came down from the tree and crawled on the picnic table.

   b) Our dog Lucky was _______ only dog wearing sunglasses at the park today.

   c) My uncle found _______ umbrella to lend me when it rained.

   d) Lars took home _______ trophy for the best track-and-field score.

9. Underline the **adjective**. Circle whether the adjective **does** or **does not** tell **exactly how many**.

   a) Many boats are docked at the marina.    *does   does not*

   b) Our cat Taffy has a litter of five kittens.    *does   does not*

   c) Mom told my sister several times to take the dog for a walk.    *does   does not*

   d) Few people are as nice and as happy as my friend Marc.    *does   does not*

10. Use the correct form of the **adjective** in brackets to **compare two** or **more than two things**.

   a) My dog is smart, but my rat is _________________. (smart)

   b) My mom is a very good cook, but my grandma is _______________. (good)

   c) That puppy is _________________ looking creature I have ever seen. (sad)

   d) Tomorrow will have _______________ weather of the whole week. (bad)

11. Underline the **action verb** in each sentence. **Do not** underline verbs that **do not** express an action.

   a) Jasper galloped around the grassy field.

   b) The cardinals flew from the cedar tree to the spruce tree.

   c) Seven birds are on the clothesline.

   d) The dog woke me up at 5:00 this morning.

12. Use the correct **present tense** or **past tense verb** for the verb in brackets.

a) The blind in the kitchen window __________ out the sun on hot days. (block)

b) When Lina is happy, she __________ everywhere. (skip)

c) Last Monday, two birds ______________ over a tree to make a nest in. (fight)

d) Yesterday, the big pot of soup __________________ on the stovetop. (simmer)

13. Circle the **helping verb** in brackets that fits best.

a) Tony ( is   am ) going to study for a test this afternoon.

b) My dad says I ( might   must ) be able to stay with my grandparents this weekend.

c) The squirrels in our tree ( was   were ) chattering noisly for some reason.

d) Mrs. Gomez ( is   was ) walking to the mailbox to get her mail now.

14. Circle whether the underlined **adverb** describes **how**, **where**, **when**, or **how often**.

a) My cousin bought a new car <u>yesterday</u>.   *how   where   when   how often*

b) Our new puppy tripped on the rug and fell <u>flat</u> on the floor.
*how   where   when   how often*

c) The mother <u>always</u> sings to her sleepy baby.   *how   where   when   how often*

d) Misty is afraid of the thunder, so she hides <u>under</u> the couch.
*how   where   when   how often*

15. Add the **correct punctuation**. Write the **sentence type** beside each sentence.

a) Oh no, I forgot my notebook___   ______________________________

b) Please try to be quieter___   ______________________________

c) Isn't that dog huge___   ______________________________

d) I did not see that coming___   ______________________________

16. Draw a vertical line between the **complete subject** and the **complete predicate**.

a) The new can opener works beautifully!

b) My dad and my brother cleaned up the yard yesterday.

c) Gerry and Ravi imagine they are famous basketball players.

d) You must pay close attention to traffic when crossing the street.

17. Write the **correct conjunction** from the words in brackets.

a) I finished my homework, _______ I have a book chapter I also need to read.
(and   but)

b) We need to go to the grocery store _______ we are out of milk and bread.
(because   since)

c) John wanted to ride to school, _______ he had to put his helmet on first. (so   or)

d) Cassie needed to wear jeans _______ working in the dirty garden. (after   while)

18. Write the **correct preposition** from the words in brackets.

a) ______________ my baby sister comes home, we will have a party. (Before   After)

b) I've felt terrible ______________ that spider crawled on my arm. (until   since)

c) I'm so tired, I wish I could lean ______________ the wall to rest. (along   against)

d) George saw that his lost pencil had fallen ______________ the bookcase.
(below   behind)

19. Add **quotation marks** and the **correct punctuation**.

a) Mr. Samms said   I can't believe my dog ate all that watermelon

b) You must remember to bring enough water to drink   warned the coach

c) Grandma asked   Would you like to see the surprise I brought for both of you

d) Don't climb on that wall   the janitor shouted

20. Circle the **correct choice** in brackets.

a) I went to see a ( doctor   Dr. )  on Hamilton ( avenue   Ave.) last Thursday.

b) Did ( doctor   Dr. ) Reddy move to her new office on Western (road   Rd. ) yet?

c) They saw ( Mister   Mr. ) Shaw at the grocery store on Barkley (St.   street ).

d) I saw a fire engine on your ( St.   street ) at ( mistress   Mrs. ) Gomez's house.

21. Add **commas** where needed.

a) Mike Emma and I went to the library this afternoon.

b) We bought carrots potatoes onions and mushrooms to make our stew.

c) I want to go hiking try fishing and swim in the lake when we go camping.

d) Marty brought strawberries apples and bananas for snacks.

22. Make the correct **contractions** from the words in brackets.

a) _____________ already run two races that day. (He had)

b) Does Amira know that _____________ found her key? (we have)

c) Our old computer _________________ work anymore. (does not)

d) The apples on the tree _________________ ripe yet. (were not)

23. Use **capital letters** where necessary to write the titles below.

a) where the wild things are _______________________________________________

b) you are my sunshine _______________________________________________

c) green eggs and ham _______________________________________________

d) giraffes can't dance _______________________________________________

e) the boxcar children _______________________________________________

f) apples and bananas _______________________________________________

# WONDERFUL WORK!

_________________________
NAME

Achievement Award – Grammar Practice Grade 4

# GREAT GRAMMAR!

_________________________
NAME

# Answers

**What Is a Noun? pp. 2–4**

1. **a)** road, television, tulip, frog **b)** uncle, banana, dentist **c)** sweater, computer, office, friend **d)** chocolate, desk, bathtub, architect, Richmond
**e)** kitchen, crystal, mountain, officer

2. **a)** Mrs. Lupino, tomatoes, garden, backyard **b)** park, children, snow **c)** Ali, parents, France, airplane **d)** father, cake, refrigerator, guests
**e)** pencil, pen, answers, questions **f)** store, fruits, vegetables

3. *Responses will vary. Sample response:* My sister saw a squirrel in the backyard.

4. Sandy enjoys walking her dog on Clark Street and in the park. She wants to start a dog-walking service in the neighborhood. Sandy asks her mother if she knows any neighbors who might be interested. They talk to Mrs. Garcia down the street and Sandy explains her idea. Mrs. Garcia says she needs help walking her dog, and Sandy has her first customer! Mom helps Sandy put a sign on the front lawn that says "Dog Walking Service." Mr. Jones comes by and asks Sandy to come to his house on Mill Street on Tuesdays. Other neighbors come by, too. Now Sandy is a very busy girl. She walks eight dogs every week!

2. Answers will vary. Ensure the adverbs describe where, how, and when correctly. You may wish to ask volunteers to share their sentences.

**Common Nouns and Proper Nouns, pp. 5–6**

1. **b)** planet **c)** street *or* road **d)** doctor **e)** month

2. **a)** Marco, Poplar Road **b)** Mayo Clinic, United States **c)** Queens Library **d)** June, Dr. Williams, Greece **e)** Neptune, Saturn **f)** Josie, Cancer Society, May **g)** Natural History Museum **h)** Eagle Elementary School; Eagle, Idaho

3. **a)** common noun **b)** proper noun **c)** common noun **d)** proper noun **e)** common noun **f)** proper noun **g)** proper noun **h)** common noun
**i)** common noun **j)** proper noun

**Exploring Proper Nouns, pp. 7–8**

1. **a)** Greenville Pet Store, Tuesday **b)** Mother's Day, Uncle George, Maine **c)** April, Mrs. Alvarez, Alamo in San Antonio, Texas **d)** New Year's Day; Columbus, Ohio

2. **a)** Rocky Mountains **b)** Peace Bridge, United States, Canada **c)** Aunt Amy, Bighorn River, Montana **d)** Maine Sluggers, Mr. Johnson's

3. Answers will vary. Ensure that capitals are used correctly.

4. Sylvia and Bob were on summer vacation. In school, they had learned all about planets such as Jupiter and Mars. Their moms decided to take them to the California Science Center so they could learn more. Bob and Sylvia lived in San Diego, California. They had to drive all the way to Los Angeles, California, to get to the California Science Center. It was worth the drive. Everyone had a great day, and Sylvia and Bob even got to pick something from the gift shop!

**Making Nouns Plural, p. 10**

**a)** boxes **b)** dishes **c)** buses **d)** speeches **e)** radishes **f)** puppies **g)** butterflies **h)** bosses **i)** ponies

**Tricky Plural Nouns, pp. 11–13**

1. **a)** tomatoes **b)** zeros **c)** videos **d)** radios

2. **a)** We watched videos about volcanoes erupting. **b)** We weighed the potatoes, but the scale showed only zeros. **c)** Kelly played solos on pianos on the patios.

3. **a)** geese **b)** mice **c)** deer

4. **a)** The children can see mice hiding in the long grass. **b)** The wives made lots of food for the people at the party. **c)** The women went to see the sheep at the fair.

5. **a)** thieves, cliffs **b)** wolves, elves **c)** scarfs, leaves

6. **a)** The boys laughed at the spoofs of their favorite movie. **b)** The chiefs ate the apple halves. **c)** Big fluffs are rolling across the living room floor.

**Singular Possessive Nouns, p. 14**

**a)** The table's legs were wobbly. **b)** Abdul's coat got wet in the rain. **c)** The bird's chirping woke me up. **d)** Will you help me find the container's lid? **e)** Anna's books are on the shelf.

**Plural Possessive Nouns, p. 15**

1. **a)** neighbors' **b)** trees' **c)** airplanes'

2. **a)** The women's coats are in the bedroom. **b)** I enjoyed hearing the children's laughter. **c)** We heard the people's shouts from far away.

**Possessive Nouns Review, p. 16**

**a)** buildings' **b)** children's **c)** students' **d)** neighborhood's **e)** flowers' **f)** farmer's **g)** boys'

## Nouns Review Quiz, pp. 17–18

**1. a)** common **b)** proper **c)** Proper

**2. b)** month **c)** state **d)** continent **e)** river

**3. a)** My dog Fritzy chewed up Saturn and Mars from my solar system set. **b)** The Natural History Museum in Los Angeles, has lots of dinosaur skeletons. **c)** My brother Troy built a model of the Space Shuttle *Discovery* for science class.

**4. a)** wishes **b)** balloons **c)** beaches

**5. a)** chefs **b)** children **c)** shelves **d)** people **e)** men, women

**6. a)** dog's hair **b)** boxers' gloves **c)** box's contents **d)** cave's secrets **e)** cats' claws **f)** People's hopes

## Exploring Pronouns, p. 19

**a)** She **b)** We **c)** I **d)** you **e)** them **f)** They **g)** it **h)** them **i)** her **j)** me **k)** us

## Should You Use *I* or *Me*? pp. 20–22

**1. a)** Luke and **I** sang two songs. Luke and I sang two songs. **b)** Mom gave the apples to Kylie and **me**. Mom gave the apples to Kylie and me. **c)** He said that Mario and **I** worked hard. He said that Mario and I worked hard. **d)** Dad asked Tamika and **me** to help. Dad asked Tamika and me to help. **e)** Mom bought Julio and **me** a new video game. Mom bought Julio and me a new video game. **f)** I wonder if you and **I** will be famous. I wonder if you and I will be famous. **g)** The magician let Cindy and **me** help him. The magician let Cindy and me help him.

**2. a)** I **b)** me **c)** I **d)** me **e)** I **f)** me **g)** I **h)** me **i)** I **j)** I

**3.** Sentences will vary. Ensure the pronoun *I* is used correctly.

**4.** Sentences will vary. Ensure the pronoun *me* is used correctly.

## Pronoun–Verb Agreement, pp. 23–24

**1. a)** writes **b)** have **c)** washes **d)** imagine **e)** creeps **f)** space **g)** have, curls **h)** see, has, is

**2. a)** has **b)** hike **c)** travel **d)** makes **e)** want **f)** feels **g)** creep **h)** snuggle **i)** leaves

## Possessive Pronouns, p. 25

**a)** yours **b)** theirs **c)** its **d)** ours **e)** his, theirs **f)** mine, hers

## Exploring Possessive Pronouns, pp. 26–27

**1. b)** mine, yours **c)** ours **d)** hers, his **e)** theirs

**2. a)** mine, I **b)** yours, you **c)** his, Jonathan **d)** hers, Samantha **e)** ours, Nina and I **f)** theirs, Monica and Abdul **g)** its, horse

**3.** Sentences will vary. Ensure the possessive pronouns are used correctly.

**4. a)** hers **b)** its **c)** their **d)** our **e)** theirs

## Pronouns Review Quiz, pp. 28–29

**1. a)** you **b)** me **c)** her **d)** it **e)** them **f)** she **g)** We, him **h)** They, us **i)** I, he

**2. a)** me **b)** I **c)** me **d)** I **e)** I **f)** me **g)** I **h)** me

3. a) wish **b)** make **c)** has **d)** rolls **e)** brush **f)** laugh **g)** have **h)** paint

4. a) My hair is curly, and yours is straight. **b)** The boy left school without his jacket. **c)** Bessie the cow could not find her baby anywhere. **d)** This week, the Brownies sold lots of their cookies.

## What Is an Adjective? p. 30

1. **a)** Circle "ancient" and underline "castle"; draw an arrow from "ancient" to "castle." **b)** Circle "funny" and underline "movie"; draw an arrow from "funny" to "movie." **c)** Circle "noisy" and underline "children"; draw an arrow from "noisy" to "children." **d)** Circle "wobbly" and underline "chair"; draw an arrow from "wobbly" to "chair." **e)** Circle "striped" and underline "sweater"; draw an arrow from "striped" to "sweater."

2. **a)** Circle "warm" and underline "water"; draw an arrow from "warm" to "water." Circle "dirty" and underline "floor"; draw an arrow from "dirty" to "floor." **b)** Circle "red" and underline "coat"; draw an arrow from "red" to "coat." Circle "cold" and underline "days"; draw an arrow from "cold" to "days." **c)** Circle "old" and underline "truck"; draw an arrow from "old" to "truck." Circle "bumpy" and underline "road"; draw an arrow from "bumpy" to "road." Circle "foggy" and underline "night"; draw an arrow from "foggy" to "night." **d)** Circle "hungry" and underline "lion"; draw an arrow from "hungry" to "lion." Circle "tall" and underline "grass"; draw an arrow from "tall" to "grass." **e)** Circle "sneaky" and underline "thieves"; draw an arrow from "sneaky" to "thieves." Circle "valuable" and underline "jewels"; draw an arrow from "valuable" to "jewels." Circle "rich" and underline "woman"; draw an arrow from "rich" to "woman." **f)** Circle "brave" and underline "astronauts"; draw an arrow from "brave" to "astronauts." Circle "fast" and underline "spaceship"; draw an arrow from "fast" to "spaceship." g) Circle "tiny" and underline "fish"; draw an arrow from "tiny" to "fish." Circle "large" and underline "aquarium"; draw an arrow from "large" to "aquarium."

## Using the Articles *A*, *An*, and *The*, pp. 31–32

**1. a)** The **b)** a **c)** an **d)** The **e)** The **f)** the **g)** a **h)** the **i)** an **j)** an **k)** an **l)** a **m)** a

## Adjectives Before and After Nouns, p. 33

**1. a)** underline "cute"; after **b)** underline "tired"; after **c)** underline "wild"; before **d)** underline "hungry"; after **e)** underline "sore"; before **f)** underline "empty"; before

**2. a)** Circle "young" and underline "magician"; draw an arrow from "young" to "magician." Circle "amazing" and underline "tricks"; draw an arrow from "amazing" to "tricks." **b)** Circle "fresh" and "delicious" and underline "muffins"; draw arrows from "fresh" and "delicious" to "muffins." **c)** Circle "long" and "boring" and underline "movie"; draw arrows from "long" and "boring" to "movie." **d)** Circle "Orange" and "yellow" and underline "leaves"; draw arrows from "Orange" and "yellow" to "leaves." Circle "old" and underline "tree"; draw an arrow from "old" to "tree." **e)** Circle "new" and underline "teacher"; draw an arrow from "new" to "teacher." Circle "red," "long," and "curly" and underline "hair"; draw arrows from "red," "long," and "curly" to "hair." **f)** Circle "nephew" and underline "Ben"; draw an arrow from "nephew" to "Ben." Circle "amazing" and underline "skier"; draw an arrow from "amazing" to "skier."

### Adjectives Can Describe How Many, p. 34
1. **a)** underline "four"; does **b)** underline "some"; does not **c)** underline "Few"; does not **d)** underline "several"; does not **e)** underline "three", does; underline "many", does not **f)** underline "All"; does not
2. **a)** Circle "old" and underline "house"; draw an arrow from "old" to "house." Circle "several" and "broken" and underline "windows"; draw arrows from "several" and "broken" to "windows." **b)** Circle "all" and underline "butterflies"; draw an arrow from "all" to "butterflies." Circle "colorful" and underline "wings"; draw an arrow from "colorful" to "wings." **c)** Circle "many" and underline "parents"; draw an arrow from "many" to "parents." Circle "some" and underline "questions"; draw an arrow from "some" to "questions." Circle "new" and underline "principal"; draw an arrow from "new" to "principal." **d)** Circle "eager" and underline "students; draw an arrow from "eager" to "students." Circle "limited" and underline "time"; draw an arrow from "limited" to "time."

### Using Adjectives to Compare Two Things, pp. 35–36
1. **a)** faster **b)** longer **c)** softer **d)** louder **e)** slower **f)** sweeter **g)** taller **h)** cooler **i)** younger **j)** cleaner **k)** rougher
2. **a)** thinner **b)** hotter **c)** redder **d)** bigger **e)** wetter **f)** sadder **g)** flatter **h)** fitter
3. **a)** rounder **b)** slimmer **c)** older **d)** dimmer **e)** harder **f)** fatter **g)** madder

### Adjectives to Compare More Than Two Things, pp. 37–38
1. **a)** sharpest; knives in the drawer **b)** youngest; children in the family **c)** tallest; all the students in his class **d)** cleanest **e)** fastest **f)** oldest
2. **a)** biggest; all the tents in the store **b)** saddest; all the movies I have seen **c)** thinnest; all the cookies on the plate **d)** flattest; all the pillows in the house **e)** hottest; all the weeks in summer so far **f)** reddest; all the cars I have ever seen **g)** wettest; all the kids who were in the water balloon fight **h)** dimmest; all stars in the known universe

### More Adjectives That Compare, p. 39
**a)** better **b)** the most **c)** farther **d)** the worst **e)** more **f)** worse **g)** the best **h)** the farthest

### Spelling Adjectives That Compare, p. 40
**a)** bumpiest **b)** riper **c)** prettiest **d)** cuter **e)** wisest **f)** sunnier **g)** fatter **h)** thinnest **i)** flatter **j)** messiest

### Adjectives and Articles Review Quiz, pp. 41–42
1. **a)** Circle "muddy" and draw an arrow from "muddy" to "boots." Circle "clean" and draw an arrow from "clean" to "floor." **b)** Circle "different" and draw an arrow from "different" to "colors." **c)** Circle "blueberry" and draw an arrow from "blueberry" to "pancakes." Circle "family" and draw an arrow from "family" to "brunch." **d)** Circle "elderly" and draw an arrow from "elderly" to "people." Circle "seniors'" and draw an arrow from "seniors'" to "home."
2. **a)** a **b)** the **c)** an, the **d)** The, the, an
3. **a)** Underline "striped"; before **b)** Underline "blue" and "purple"; after **c)** Underline "messy" and "delicious"; after **d)** Underline "long" and "difficult"; before
4. **a)** Underline "Many"; does not **b)** Underline "five"; does **c)** Underline "several"; does not **d)** Underline "four"; does
5. **a)** faster **b)** wettest **c)** better **d)** longer **e)** flatter
6. **a)** the coldest **b)** the best **c)** the highest **d)** the slowest
7. **a)** fluffier, the fluffiest **b)** larger, the largest **c)** the best **d)** the shadiest **e)** riper **f)** the worst **g)** the farthest

### Action Verbs, p. 43
**a)** attended **b)** eats **c)** wiped **d)** no action verb **e)** echoes **f)** went **g)** giggled **h)** grew **i)** skis **j)** told **k)** fixed **l)** searches

### Linking Verbs, pp. 44–45
1. **a)** excited; an adjective **b)** scared; an adjective **c)** cashier; a noun **d)** restless; adjective **e)** veteran; noun
2. **a)** feel **b)** tastes **c)** became **d)** is **e)** sounds **f)** looks **g)** was **h)** stay

### Exploring Present Tense Verbs, pp. 46–47
1. **a)** return **b)** waits **c)** heats **d)** climb
2. **a)** Mom **b)** They **c)** Angelo **d)** He
3. **a)** Tracey **b)** The kittens **c)** The tree **d)** The people
4. **a)** eat **b)** dances **c)** walks **d)** have **e)** play **f)** makes **g)** deliver
5. **a)** Cindy **b)** They **c)** Trisha **d)** My friends **e)** basketball **f)** My uncle **g)** Kelly and Kim **h)** No one

### Exploring Past Tense Verbs, pp. 48–49
1. **a)** talked **b)** poured **c)** walked **d)** mixed **e)** played **f)** fixed **g)** danced **h)** created **i)** smelled **j)** jumped
2. **a)** I walked to school with my friends. **b)** I fixed the mistakes I made on my homework. **c)** My sister played the fiddle at the competition.
3. **a)** past tense **b)** past tense **c)** present tense **d)** past tense **e)** present tense **f)** past tense **g)** present tense
4. **a)** aimed **b)** hammered **c)** helped **d)** learned **e)** repaired **f)** melted **g)** lifted

     

## Tricky Past Tense Verbs, p. 50

**a)** drove **b)** gave **c)** got **d)** ate **e)** came, had **f)** fell **g)** had **h)** drank **i)** took **j)** went

## Exploring Future Tense Verbs, p. 51

**a)** will come **b)** will walk **c)** will play **d)** will run **e)** will read **f)** will jump **g)** will eat **h)** will drink **i)** will help **j)** will learn **k)** will change **l)** will travel

## Helping Verbs for Future Tense, p. 52

**a)** could **b)** can **c)** should **d)** may **e)** should **f)** Could **g)** May **h)** might **i)** would **j)** should **k)** might **l)** can

## Using *May*, *Might*, and *Must* as Helping Verbs, p. 53

**a)** must, probably true **b)** must, required or necessary **c)** may, permission **d)** must, probably true **e)** might, possible action **f)** must, required or necessary, **g)** may, possible action

## Using *Am*, *Is*, and *Are* as Helping Verbs, p. 54

**a)** is mowing **b)** are barking **c)** is ringing **d)** are walking **e)** are falling **f)** is fixing **g)** am listening **h)** is being **i)** are being **j)** am being **k)** are being

## Using *Was* and *Were* as Helping Verbs, p. 55

**1. a)** were playing **b)** was looking **c)** were reading **d)** were watching **e)** was sleeping
**2. a)** The man was walking home when he slipped. **b)** Tina was working when Frank called her. **c)** I was looking for my hat when you found it.

## Spelling Verbs That End with *ing*, p. 56

**1. a)** giving **b)** dividing **c)** hoping **d)** inviting **e)** dying **f)** untying **g)** running **h)** sitting **i)** jogging **j)** rowing **k)** fixing **l)** cutting **m)** saying **n)** winning
**2. a)** skiing **b)** getting **c)** shaking **d)** enjoying **e)** seeing **f)** stopping

## Verbs Review Quiz, pp. 57–58

**1. a)** groomed **b)** swim, escape **c)** called, arrive **d)** know
**2. a)** smells; noun **b)** are; noun **c)** feel; adjective **d)** seems; adjective
**3. a)** reads **b)** sleeps **c)** swims **d)** giggles **e)** borrows **f)** dives
**4. a)** made **b)** helped **c)** sat **d)** coiled
**5. a)** will **b)** must **c)** may **d)** must
**6. a)** is studying **b)** are grooming **c)** am going **d)** is carrying
**7. a)** was watering **b)** were walking **c)** was dreaming **d)** were crawling

## Some Adverbs Describe How, p. 60

**1. a)** Circle "loudly" and underline "spoke"; draw an arrow from "loudly" to "spoke." **b)** Circle "swiftly" and underline "flew"; draw an arrow from "swiftly" to "flew." **c)** Circle "gently" and underline "rocks"; draw an arrow from "gently" to "rocks." **d)** Circle "carefully" and underline "checked"; draw an arrow from "carefully" to "checked." **e)** Circle "politely" and underline " asked"; draw an arrow from "politely" to "asked." **f)** Circle "neatly" and underline "writes"; draw an arrow from "neatly" to "writes." **g)** Circle "angrily" and underline "shouted"; draw an arrow from "angrily" to "shouted." **h)** Circle "mysteriously" and underline "vanished"; draw an arrow from "mysteriously" to "vanished."
**2. a)** Suddenly, brightly **b)** Slowly, silently **c)** softly, calmly

## Some Adverbs Describe When, p. 61

**a)** Circle "tonight" and underline "watch"; draw an arrow from "tonight" to "watch." **b)** Circle "now" and underline "swim"; draw an arrow from "now" to "swim." **c)** Circle "Yesterday" and underline "wrapped"; draw an arrow from "Yesterday" to "wrapped." **d)** Circle "late" and underline "arrived"; draw an arrow from "late" to "arrived." **e)** Circle "soon" and underline "melt"; draw an arrow from "soon" to "melt." **f)** Circle "frequently" and underline "drink"; draw an arrow from "frequently" to "drink." **g)** Circle "last" and underline "finished"; draw an arrow from "last" to "finished." **h)** Circle "Next" and underline "read"; draw an arrow from "Next" to "read." **i)** Circle "before" and underline "call"; draw an arrow from "before" to "call."

## Some Adverbs Describe Where, p. 62

**1. a)** Circle "here" and underline "hang"; draw an arrow from "here" to "hang." **b)** Circle "nearby" and underline "found"; draw an arrow from "nearby" to "found." **c)** Circle "everywhere" and underline "looked"; draw an arrow from "everywhere" to "looked." **d)** Circle "downstairs" and underline "took"; draw an arrow from "downstairs" to "took." **e)** Circle "anywhere" and underline "put"; draw an arrow from "anywhere" to "put." **f)** Circle "outside" and underline "go"; draw an arrow from "outside" to "go." **g)** Circle "there" and underline "hung"; draw an arrow from "there" to "hung." **h)** Circle "outdoors" and underline "ate"; draw an arrow from "outdoors" to "ate."
**2. a)** outside, indoors **b)** east, west

## Exploring Adverbs That Describe How Where and When, p. 63

**1.** I walked <u>quickly</u> (toward) my school. I slept in [late today] and did not want to miss my math test. When I [finally] arrived at school, my teacher looked <u>seriously</u> at me and asked, "Why are you [late] Jonathan?" I looked (inside) the classroom. My classmates were all (there) <u>quietly</u> writing their tests. I <u>nervously</u> answered my teacher and explained that I had <u>accidentally</u> slept in. She asked me to get a late slip [first], and to hurry (back) [after] so I could write my test.

**Some Adverbs Describe How Often, p. 64**

1. **a)** Circle "often," underline "visits"; draw an arrow from "often" to "visits." **b)** Circle "sometimes," underline :play"; draw an arrow from "sometimes" to "play." **c)** Circle "never," underline "forget"; draw an arrow from "never" to "forget." **d)** Circle "twice," underline "sneezed"; draw an arrow from "twice" to "sneezed."
2. **a)** constantly **b)** seldom **c)** rarely **d)** Occasionally **e)** frequently **f)** Usually

**Adverbs Review Quiz, pp. 65–66**

1. **a)** quickly **b)** brightly **c)** boldly, politely **d)** timidly, slowly
2. **a)** after, this evening **b)** yesterday, today **c)** last summer **d)** this weekend
3. **a)** inside, all over **b)** worldwide **c)** throughout, anywhere **d)** upstairs, underneath **e)** below, inside
4. **a)** sometimes **b)** always **c)** fifty-five times **d)** never, once
5. **a)** frequently **b)** occasionally **c)** rarely **d)** usually
6. **a)** how often **b)** how **c)** where **d)** how often **e)** how **f)** when **g)** where **h)** when

**Exploring Types of Sentence, pp. 67–69**

1. **a)** question mark **b)** period **c)** exclamation mark **d)** question mark **e)** period **f)** exclamation mark **g)** question mark **h)** period
2. Sentences will vary. Ensure the correct type of sentence and correct punctuation are used.
3. **a)** exclamation **b)** question **c)** statement **d)** exclamation **e)** command **f)** statement **g)** question **h)** command **i)** statement

**Complete Subjects, pp. 70–71**

1. **a) The red car b)** Millions of stars **c)** The girl with the broken leg **d)** Our friends from Halifax **e)** The bread my mother made **f)** Sasha's speech about the solar system **g)** The long-haired dog **h)** The busy squirrels **i)** The strap on Terry's backpack
2. A vertical line should be drawn after the following words: **a)** school **b)** meatballs **c)** pie **d)** garden **e)** composter **f)** bats **g)** whales
3. **a)** Yes **b)** No **c)** No **d)** Yes **e)** Yes **f)** No **g)** Yes **h)** Yes

**Complete Predicates, pp. 72–73**

1. Underline the following: **a)** tasted delicious **b)** watched the fireworks last night **c)** swam together in the ocean **d)** watch cartoons on Saturday mornings **e)** make running easier **f)** leans against the brick wall **g)** ripen in the middle of summer **h)** grow between the toes of my friend's fluffy cat
2. A vertical line should be drawn before the following words: **a)** can **b)** eat **c)** drink **d)** cross **e)** provide **f)** eat **g)** find
3. **a)** Yes **b)** No **c)** Yes **d)** No **e)** No **f)** Yes **g)** Yes **h)** No

**Avoiding Sentence Fragments, pp. 74–76**

1. **a)** the action **b)** who or what is doing the action **c)** both are missing **d)** the action **e)** who or what is doing the action **f)** both are missing
2. **a)** sentence fragment **b)** sentence **c)** sentence fragment **d)** sentence fragment **e)** sentence **f)** sentence fragment
3. Answers will vary. You may wish to ask volunteers to share their sentences with the class.
4. Cross out the following: **a)** and his dog. **b)** and I. **c)** on the shelf. **d)** notebook and pen.

**Avoiding Run-On Sentences, pp. 77–78**

1. **a)** run-on sentence **b)** run-on sentence **c)** run-on sentence **d)** check mark **e)** run-on sentence **f)** run-on sentence
2. **a)** I forgot my pencil. I have another one.; I forgot my pencil, but I have another one. **b)** The dog is outside. It needs to come in.; The dog is outside, and it needs to come in. **c)** My sister washed the dishes. I dried them.; My sister washed the dishes, and I dried them.

**Conjunctions: *And, But, Or,* and *So,* p. 79**

1. **a)** and **b)** but **c)** but **d)** and
2. **a)** or **b)** so **c)** so **d)** or

**Conjunctions: *Since, Because, Until, Before, After, While, When,* and *As Soon As,* p. 80**

**a)** when **b)** until **c)** after **d)** as soon as **e)** while **f)** because

**Prepositions, p. 81**

**a)** to **b)** from **c)** *in* **d)** with **e)** by **f)** at **g)** on **h)** for **i)** before **j)** around

**Sentences Review Quiz, pp. 82–83**

1. **a)** Add a period; command **b)** Add a question mark; question **c)** Add a period; statement **d)** Add an exclamation mark; exclamation
2. Vertical line should be between the following words: **a)** geese eating **b)** mouse chewed **c)** elephants shows **d)** drawer sticks
3. **a)** sentence fragment **b)** sentence **c)** sentence fragment **d)** sentence
4. **a)** run-on sentence **b)** run-on sentence **c)** run-on sentence **d)** check mark
5. **a)** so **b)** but **c)** and **d)** or
6. **a)** while **b)** when **c)** as soon as **d)** after
7. **a)** After **b)** between **c)** from **d)** along

 

**Punctuating Dialogue, pp. 84–86**

**1. a)** "We won the game!" shouted Mary. **b)** "I hope we have good weather during our vacation," Dad said. **c)** "I wonder if she noticed that we came in late," whispered Beth. **d)** "Would you like to look through the telescope?" asked the scientist. **e)** The police officer said, "We have caught the thief." **f)** "Does he know we are following him?" asked the spy. **g)** The children said, "We always have fun at the beach." **h)** Aaron nervously said, "The wind has really picked up!" **i)** Leann exclaimed, "That new haircut looks great on you!"

**2. a)** "That bird flew right over my head!" shouted Yu. **b)** Danny asked, "Does anyone know where the scrap paper is kept?" **c)** Miss Henry said, "Open your books and turn to page 19." **d)** "Sand is stuck all over me!" complained Minnie. **e)** Mom warned, "Make sure you look both ways before you cross the street." **f)** "I have an idea for a Father's Day gift for Dad," Kevin whispered. **g)** "How is Benny feeling today?" Mrs. Martinez asked Mom.

**3. a)** "Have you seen the new skateboard Ashley got?" asked Todd. **b)** "Move away from the door," Mom said to our dog. **c)** Karen groaned, "I have so much homework to do." **d)** "I won the spelling bee!" Tim announced. **e)** Cathy asked, "Why is this door open?" **f)** "That cloud looks like a teddy bear!" said May. **g)** "Can anyone tell us the answer?" asked Mrs. Turnbull. **h)** Amy whispered, "Do you see the baby birds in the nest on that branch?" **i)** Mr. Green said, "Please help me carry these packages to the car."

**Abbreviations, pp. 87–88**

**1. a)** Dr. **b)** road **c)** St. **d)** avenue **e)** Dr., doctor **f)** Rd. **g)** street **h)** Ave.

**2. a)** <u>Dr.</u> Lindzon spoke at a seminar with <u>Mrs.</u> Lopez. **b)** check mark **c)** How close is Waterside <u>Rd.</u> to the office where <u>Mr.</u> Castle works? **d)** Are there lots of trees on your <u>street</u>?

**Using Commas in Lists, p. 89**

**1. a)** Brady's favorite snacks are bananas, crackers, and cheese. **b)** My favorite shirt has blue, green, and yellow stripes. **c)** Andrew, Evan, and Ella are in the Environment Club. **d)** Wednesday, Thursday, and Friday are track and field practice days. **e)** Emma asked Emile, Sheena, and Leo to come over after school. **f)** My parents like to play in tennis, volleyball, and soccer leagues.

**2. a)** Hanna washed the car, cut the grass, and took out the garbage. **b)** The bird flew over the fence, across the yard, and into the maple tree **c)** My sister, my brother, and I helped to shovel the snow. **d)** I spend most of my time attending school, doing homework, and playing with my friends. **e)** Eat breakfast, get enough sleep, and exercise to stay healthy. **f)** I want to finish my homework, play outside, and call my friend before bedtime.

**Contractions with *Have* and *Had*, p. 90**

**a)** I've **b)** She'd **c)** they've **d)** we'd **e)** I'd **f)** you've **g)** they'd

**Contractions with *Not*, p. 91**

**a)** mustn't **b)** wouldn't **c)** hadn't **d)** won't **e)** shouldn't **f)** couldn't **g)** haven't **h)** can't **i)** aren't

**Using *There*, *Their*, and *They're*, p. 92**

**a)** Their **b)** They're **c)** there **d)** they're **e)** there **f)** their **g)** there **h)** their **i)** They're, their **j)** their, they're **k)** They're, there

**Using Capital Letters in Titles, p. 93**

**1. a)** James and the Giant Peach **b)** Dancing in the Street **c)** The Indian in the Cupboard **d)** The Wizard of Oz **e)** A Chair for My Mother **f)** Down by the Lake

**2.** Book and movie titles will vary. You may wish to ask students to share with the class.

**Write the Correct Word, p. 94**

**a)** than **b)** its **c)** may be **d)** then **e)** it's **f)** than **g)** It's, its **h)** Maybe, may be

**Correcting Errors: *Boa Constrictors*, p. 95**

*Paragraph 1, sentence 2:* <u>It</u> <u>is</u> one of the longest snakes in the world.

*Paragraph 1, sentence 4:* <u>Boas</u> live in the wild in warm countries such as <u>Mexico</u>.

*Paragraph 1, sentence 6:* They feel that looking after a boa is easier <u>than</u> looking after other kinds of pets.

*Paragraph 2, sentence 1:* Most boas have skin that <u>is</u> different shades of brown.

*Paragraph 2, sentence 2:* The colors on their skin help boas hide among dead <u>leaves</u> on the ground.

*Paragraph 2, sentence 3:* Boas have different patterns on <u>their</u> skin.

*Paragraph 2, sentence 4:* One scientist <u>said,</u> "<u>They're</u> beautiful animals.

*Paragraph 2, sentence 5:* I think boas have the most interesting patterns of all <u>snakes."</u>

*Paragraph 3, sentence 1:* A boa kills its prey by wrapping itself around an <u>animal's</u> body.

*Paragraph 3, sentence 3:* <u>It</u> (or "<u>The boa</u>") squeezes so tight the animal <u>can't</u> breathe.

*Paragraph 4, sentence 1:* If a boa hisses, that means it <u>may be</u> angry.

*Paragraph 4, sentence 2:* <u>You'd</u> better be careful if a boa hisses at you.

*Paragraph 4, sentence 3:* Boas are not <u>poisonous</u>, but they can still bite!

**Correcting Errors: *A New Stew*, p. 96**

*Paragraph 1, sentence 1:* One day, Dad and I <u>were</u> at the grocery store.
*Paragraph 1, sentence 3:* "Do you think <u>Fred</u> will like <u>this?</u>" he asked. *(delete comma)*
*Paragraph 2, sentence 2:* "<u>I'm</u> sure he'll love it."
*Paragraph 2, sentence 3:* Dad put the tin in the shopping cart with the other <u>groceries</u>.
*Paragraph 3, sentence 2:* It looked strange, and it smelled even worse <u>than</u> it looked.
*Paragraph 4, sentence 1:* "This is the <u>smelliest</u> stew <u>ever!</u>" I said. *(delete comma)*
*Paragraph 5, sentence 2:* I could tell from his face that he <u>didn't</u> like it.
*Paragraph 6, sentence 1:* "What kind of stew is <u>this?</u>" he asked Mom.
*Paragraph 7, sentence 2:* "<u>It's</u> called Beefy <u>Stew,</u>" she said.
*Paragraph 7, sentence 3:* Dad and <u>I</u> couldn't stop laughing.
*Paragraph 8, sentence 1:* Fred <u>had</u> a good dinner that night.

**Vocabulary Review 1, p. 98**

**1. a)** recent **b)** vacant **c)** accurate **d)** impact **e)** descend **f)** eager **g)** flexible
**2. a)** accurate **b)** recent **c)** eager **d)** vacant **e)** impact **f)** descended **g)** flexible

**Vocabulary Review 2, p. 100**

**1. a)** frantic **b)** reveal **c)** lack **d)** blend **e)** peculiar **f)** assist **g)** blend
**2. a)** blended **b)** peculiar **c)** lacked **d)** revealed **e)** blend **f)** assist **g)** frantic

**Vocabulary Review 3, p. 102**

**1. a)** frequent **b)** increase **c)** tidy **d)** release **e)** increase **f)** sturdy **g)** outstanding
**2. a)** tidy **b)** sturdy **c)** increase **d)** frequent **e)** outstanding **f)** release **g)** increase

**Vocabulary Review 4, p. 104**

**1. a)** severe **b)** resist **c)** queasy **d)** recognize **e)** prefer **f)** dusk **g)** portion
**2. a)** portion **b)** recognized **c)** prefers **d)** dusk **e)** queasy **f)** severe **g)** resist

**Vocabulary Review 5, p. 106**

**1. a)** jagged **b)** indicate **c)** variety **d)** sole **e)** distract **f)** source
**2. a)** indicate **b)** variety **c)** jagged **d)** source **e)** distracted **f)** soles

**Grammar Review Test Gr 4 Answers, pp. 107–112**

**1. a)** Circle "Joey," "Sari," and "Ahmad"; underline "day," "zoo," and "families" **b)** "Guggenheim Museum," "New York"; underline "artworks" and "artists" **c)** Circle "Pastor Henry," "Anglican"; underline "church" and "river" **d)** Circle "Tuesdays" and "Lucky Mart"; underline "groceries" and "street"
**2. a)** peaches **b)** fairies, troll, elves **c)** leaves, piles **d)** chefs, ladies
**3. a)** kittens' paws **b)** mouse's footprints **c)** book's pages **d)** trees' leaves
**4. a)** them **b)** they **c)** us **d)** she
**5. a)** I **b)** me **c)** me **d)** I
**6. a)** play **b)** plans **c)** help **d)** crashes
**7. a)** theirs **b)** hers **c)** his **d)** mine, yours
**8. a)** A **b)** the **c)** an **d)** the
**9. a)** Many; does not **b)** five; does **c)** several; does not **d)** few; does not
**10. a)** smarter **b)** better **c)** the saddest **d)** the worst
**11. a)** galloped **b)** flew **c)** no action verb **d)** woke
**12. a)** blocks **b)** skips **c)** fought **d)** simmered
**13. a)** is **b)** might **c)** were **d)** is
**14. a)** when **b)** how **c)** how often **d)** where
**15. a)** Add an exclamation mark; exclamation **b)** Add a period; command **c)** Add a question mark; question **d)** Add a period; statement
**16.** Draw a vertical line between the following words: **a)** opener works **b)** brother cleaned **c)** Ravi imagine **d)** must pay
**17. a)** but **b)** and **c)** so **d)** or
**18. a)** After **b)** since **c)** against **d)** behind
**19. a)** Mr. Samms said, "I can't believe my dog ate all that watermelon!" **b)** "You must remember to bring enough water to drink," warned the coach. **c)** Grandma asked, "Would you like to see the surprise I brought for both of you? **d)** "Don't climb on that wall!" the janitor shouted.
**20. a)** doctor, Ave. **b)** Dr., Rd. **c)** Mr., St. **d)** street, Mrs.
**21. a)** Mike, Emma, and I went to the library this afternoon. **b)** We bought carrots, potatoes, onions, and mushrooms to make our stew. **c)** I want to go hiking, try fishing, and swim in the lake when we go camping. **d)** Marty brought strawberries, apples, and bananas for snacks.
**22. a)** He'd **b)** we've **c)** doesn't **d)** weren't
**23. a)** Where the Wild Things Are **b)** You Are My Sunshine **c)** Green Eggs and Ham **d)** Giraffes Can't Dance **e)** The Boxcar Children **f)** Apples and Bananas